ARE YOU MAKING LOVE OR JUST HAVING SEX?

ARE YOU MAKING LOVE OR JUST HAVING SEX?

A PHILOSOPHICAL GUIDE TO ENDURING LOVE AND SEXUAL INTIMACY

ELLIOT D. COHEN, Ph.D.

ANTHEM PRESS

Anthem Press
An imprint of Wimbledon Publishing Company
www.anthempress.com

This edition first published in UK and USA 2025
by ANTHEM PRESS
75–76 Blackfriars Road, London SE1 8HA, UK
or PO Box 9779, London SW19 7ZG, UK
and
244 Madison Ave #116, New York, NY 10016, USA

© Elliot D. Cohen 2025

The author asserts the moral right to be identified as the author of this work.

All rights reserved. Without limiting the rights under copyright reserved above,
no part of this publication may be reproduced, stored or introduced into
a retrieval system, or transmitted, in any form or by any means
(electronic, mechanical, photocopying, recording or otherwise),
without the prior written permission of both the copyright
owner and the above publisher of this book.

British Library Cataloguing-in-Publication Data
A catalogue record for this book is available from the British Library.

Library of Congress Cataloging-in-Publication Data
A catalog record for this book has been requested.
2024938501

ISBN-13: 978-1-83999-235-3 (Hbk)
ISBN-10: 1-83999-235-2 (Hbk)
ISBN-13: 978-1-83999-236-0 (Pbk)
ISBN-10: 1-83999-236-0 (Pbk)

This title is also available as an e-book.

In Memory of Albert Ellis,
who always wanted to write a book on romantic love.

CONTENTS

Preface   ix

Introduction   1
Chapter 1   Building Serenity in Romantic Love   17
Chapter 2   Building Intimacy Through Empathy in Romantic Love   33
Chapter 3   Building Self-Respect and Respect for Others in Romantic Love   53
Chapter 4   Building Self-Control in Romantic Love   77
Chapter 5   Building Courage in Romantic Love   109
Chapter 6   The Ideal of Enduring Love and Sexual Intimacy   141

Index   151

PREFACE

Romantic Love and Sexual Intimacy

This book addresses the pervasive forlornness about the seeming inability to fall deeply in love. It probes the haunting sense of some unknown element of interpersonal resonance missing; the feeling as though you may be on the precipices of a great love that never seems to take flight. Indeed, many people feel in their hearts that there are the seeds of such a love, the ungerminated potential, if only the right nutrients in ample amounts were added. Some have attained sexual gratification before but still feel like there is something missing in their love life. Some feel a lamentable void in their sex life, an anxiety that gnaws at the very prospect of sexual intimacy. And some are in relationships that seem to go nowhere with a dry mechanical interchange of bodily fluids, sadly missing the magic that has so often been associated with true love.

This book identifies the underlying cognitive–behavioral dysfunctionality that feeds such incomplete relationships, and it uses philosophy to show how to remediate them. It is about romantic love, the kind of love that is intertwined with sexual intimacy. Love has many faces. It is manifested in parental love; deep bonds of friendship; Platonic love; sibling love; and the love of a close knit family. But the intimacy of romantic love is sui generis. It is a coalescence or unity of body and spirit, a sharing of identities, that has a special irreducible quality not inherent in any other form of love. Indeed, from antiquity to date, it has been the province of great works of art, literature, and religion. But, it can also be elusive and sometimes deeply painful. It can manifest itself in scorn, be engulfed in flames of rage; and silently, imperceptibly, fade away. Like a child, love can grow and mature over the years; but, also like a child, it requires care and guidance lest it become dysfunctional and stunted.

Romantic love is an intimate practice that has cognitive, behavioral, and emotional components coalescing in habits to think, feel, and act in ways that are both loving and lovable. It is aspirational in character and is therefore always a work in progress. The ideals of love, its "lovable goals," are noble, and manifest themselves in such virtues as empathy, courage, respect, self-control, and serenity; so, it is transformative of the person one is, and who one aspires to become.

As a philosophical practitioner, I have spent most of my adult life teaching, consulting, and writing about the pitfalls that undermine human relationships and what people can do to overcome these human tendencies. Having been in the trenches, both personally and professionally, I know well how painful love can be. There are both highs and lows of any relationship born this side of heaven. True love is never easy, but oh so deep is this love that couples in such a relationship would not, never for a moment, choose different mates even if they were to live their lives ten thousand times over. This love, this fragile child that matures, is never perfect; nor are the circumstances under which it flourishes; nor is it always rational and kind. But the irreducible, indissoluble bond of love that unites those in love grows progressively stronger over the years.

This book will:

1. Identify the major cognitive–behavioral obstructions that prevent the forging of such a deep, enduring bond.
2. Show how these obstacles can be overcome by changing the way you think and respond to the inevitable situations and vicissitudes of your interpersonal relations. This transformation involves a conceptual shift from well-entrenched, ineffectual goals to ones that adorn a relationship with a coalescent vitality—empathy, respect, serenity, self-control, and courage, instead of self-centeredness, conditional acceptance, self-defeating perfectionism, and needless anxiety-producing fears.
3. Demonstrate how the wisdom of the sages can produce "love philosophies" that can cultivate an authentic, enduring love. Indeed, philosophers from Plato and Buddha to Jean-Paul Sartre and Simon de Beauvoir have enlightened us about the nature of love and how to attain it.
4. Show how this wisdom can be applied toward the development of a cognitive-behavioral approach to making constructive changes in your life.

For example, the Dalai Lama counsels those whose relationships suffer from self-absorbed disregard for the often-times painful subjectivity of others, to cultivate compassion, which, he says, is "an empathetic altruism that actively strives to free others from suffering" (Dalai Lama, 2005, 49). This involves tuning out your own painful consciousness and tuning in that of your partner. It involves a nonjudgmental, caring attitude in which mundane issues that separate both of you vanish. Indeed, in this state of resonance, your own suffering evaporates, and a condition of deep, unified love can take its place. Still, as a human being, with physical needs and desires, you can never be completely altruistic. Veritably, a human being must eat, sleep, and tend to the mundane issues of life, so that consciousness must, out of practical necessity, direct itself elsewhere, away from your partner's state of mind. Thus, the actual goal is a harmonious, artful balance between personal concerns and those of your partner, moving delicately back and forth, now and then, without giving undue weight to yourself. This requires perseverance, and a lifetime commitment, with the understanding that, as a human being, you can still never be perfect. Indeed, it is an ideal toward which to aspire, but never fully realized, at least here on earth.

So enduring, authentic love is itself an aspirational ideal that flows from other ideals; always a work in progress, intertwined with growing pains, moving gradually, steadily toward a goal immeasurable in worth, fulfilling to the core. It is a love shared by two whose hearts beat harmoniously as one; yet whose freedom and dignity, as spontaneous and creative individuals, complement their unity.

Throughout history, acclaimed artists and poets, from Rembrandt to Shakespeare, have used their respective media to capture the ineffable quality of this special bond. Esteemed psychologists, from Freud to Fromm, have attempted to identify its roadblocks. Great sages, from Plato to Sartre, have added their positive guidance in aspiring to be in love. This book amalgamates the potent philosophical ideas behind this remarkable journey.

I have also included a video presentation, with a link, in each respective chapter, as well as practice guidelines and exercises, to help you in your quest. I truly hope this package helps to ignite the flames of love, burning passionately, inside and outside the bedroom, in an ever-evolving, enduring, romantic love.

Elliot D. Cohen, PhD

Reference

Dalai Lama. 2005. Essence of the Heart Sutra: The Dalai Lama's Heart of Wisdom Teachings. Trans. G. T. Jinpa. Somerville, MA: Wisdom Publications.

INTRODUCTION

WHAT DOES BEING IN LOVE REALLY INVOLVE?

Stories abound about how someone thought they were falling in love only to find out they really didn't even like the person. Indeed, sexual attraction can be intoxicating, clouding one's standards of judgment. Suddenly, a brief encounter with someone who turns one on can have the tantalizing semblance of falling in love. This is not to deny that romantic love always begins with strong sexual attraction, but the real thing is a lot more, a whole lot more, than sexual allure.

Falling in love marks the beginning of a process that evolves over time. While this beginning is one of sexual arousal, it is also a time of soul searching. The latter consists of wonderment about whether this person is "the right" one. This is especially challenging when sexual desire is at concert pitch, so one may be inclined to overlook signs to the contrary. For example, the person in question may be self-absorbed, display a lack of empathy, or behave irresponsibly, but you manage to make excuses for this person, and then convince yourself of them. Such a state gives rise to the hackneyed expression that "love is blind" when it may be more accurate to say that "sexual desire," not love, is blind.

The Import of Saying "I love You"

The words, "I love you" are typically spoken at some point in the ever-evolving process of love, marking a milestone. These three words are not merely an account of sexual attraction for the subject of pronouncement. They are uttered with a similar solemnity as the words, "I do" in a marriage ceremony; for *in* this intimate act of speech, one *makes a commitment* to be there for the one to whom one pledges one's love. This portends a commitment to care about this special person and to be prepared to make substantial personal sacrifices to promote the welfare and happiness of the beloved. "I love you, it's in my power to be there for you, but just don't count on it" carries its disingenuousness on its face; for, short of death or other impenetrable barrier, uttering these three sacred words makes a commitment of devotion to this special person. "I love you too" seals this commitment with the reciprocity that love requires, lest it be squandered on another.

Of course, friends are there for one another in times of need; so are colleagues and co-workers. So, "being there" has a distinct meaning when the commitment of love is pronounced. This is a heart-felt pledge of intimacy, a spiritual bond that can only find expression in metaphors like "My heart beats for you"; "I am eternally yours"; and "You are everything to me." This means that the joy of the beloved is one's own joy, and the suffering of the beloved, is one's own. This regard is no mere means to an end beyond the beloved's welfare and freedom from pain. For the true lover, these are intrinsically desirable ends, not something to cash in on like poker chips.

Some people are afraid to utter these words even though they want to. They may not seem to find the right moment, or they may not be certain this person is right for them. They may not be sure they are ready to settle down, or they may fear not having the pledge reciprocated. They may be waiting for the other to say these words first, or they may be afraid speaking these words might spoil a good thing, as goes the classic Sinatra tune, "And then I go and spoil it all by saying something stupid like: 'I love you.'"

Indeed, it would be ill-advised to declare one's love when one is not ready to do so; but waiting for the ideal time for anything on earth is also ill-advised. The time when one is certain may never arrive; for there may always be some doubts about the time, place, and person to whom to pledge one's love. Demanding perfection will get you nowhere! This is one extreme to avoid. At the other extreme, is willy-nilly pledging your love for another. Sadly, there are empty pronouncements of love conjured up from the visceral surges of hormones, mere infatuation, dependency or co-dependency, fear of being alone, or want of a "trophy" to possess. The right reason for pledging your love for another is because this is the person with whom you wish to share yourself in the most intimate and personal ways. So, what does it really mean to *be* in love?

True Love Ways

The deep meaning of being in love is delicately intimated in the words of this tender love song by Buddy Holly:

> Throughout the days our true love ways
> Will bring us joys to share with those who really care

Sometimes we'll sigh
Sometimes we'll cry
And we'll know why just you and I know true love ways

True love is, indeed, for "those who really care." There is no pretense behind this relationship, no thin veneer of idol words stained by stillborn commitments, missed dates, excessive excuses, deception, and unfaithfulness. It is also not the bland commitment enshrined in the language of contract, duty, or obligation. True lovers do not force themselves into compliance because they are "supposed to." On the contrary, they are there for their lover because they really care. "I love thee to the depth and breadth and height my soul can reach" spoke British Victorian poet Elizabeth Barrett Browning in counting the ways she loved thee. This is not just a fleeting feeling aroused by hormonal swings. Indeed, the feelings of love are the adornments of a passionate caring that reaches to the depths of one's soul, or beyond, enduring through even the most challenging of times. Indeed, "sometimes we'll sigh" and "sometimes we'll cry" when "you and I know true love ways." For the vicissitudes of life for those in love both challenge and strengthen the relationship. Conflict is inevitable as no relationship steeped in human passion can be perfectly harmonious. Indeed, as discussed later, the demand for perfection stifles the cognitive, emotional, and behavioral juices that coalesce in the bond of love.

Exploring Love Through Song

1. I have just given an example of how Buddy Holly's classic, "True Love Ways," might be used to unpack the meaning of love. In the following video (link provided), I have arranged, performed, and elaborated further on the lyrics of Buddy Holly's classic love song. Listen to it, think about it, and see if you can draw out more key thoughts about "true love ways"!
http://bit.ly/3vl71k0
2. I have always found that music is a wonderful segue into *feeling* the emotions expressed by the synergy of music and lyrics! Do you have a favorite love song? Listen to it and see if you can feel the emotions it expresses through blending music and lyrics. Then, while resonating with this song, try writing down some of your own thoughts it provokes, like I did with Buddy Holly's tune.

Making Love versus Just Having Sex

This magnificent bond forged in the intimacy of romantic love comes to a climax in the sexual encounter. However, the sexual encounter of "making love" is not *just* the orgasmic stimulation of sex organs. This is, in no way, to degrade the experiential value of just having sex, no more than it is to degrade having a cold beer on a hot summer day as distinct from having a glass of fine wine while dining in an intimate setting. They are *sui generis*. Both have their time and place.

Each is ensconced in distinct values, the former in hedonism while the latter in the bodily expression of virtue. For, to make love is the fruit of an authentic sharing, borne of orgasmic sexual synergy coalescing with peaceful serenity, empathy, courage, self-control, and mutual, reflexive respect and caring. It is, therefore, very special, indeed, and much less common than just having sex. It is a union of two bodily instantiated souls, transcending the mere corporeal, representing an ineffable, sublime intimacy.

The experience has the grandeur and solemnity of a deeply religious or spiritual encounter, not unlike that expressed by Neo-Platonist Plotinus (1956) in speaking of his own mystical experience of being one with the divine. "Many times it has happened," he says, "beholding a marvelous beauty; then, more than ever assured of community with the loftiest order; enacting the noblest life, acquiring identity with the divine [...]" (ennead 4, tract. 8, ch. 1, p. 357). But such an ascent is only possible, he maintains, when one has worked hard to purify one's soul, building virtuous habits of wisdom, justice, courage, and temperance. The conditions of making love are not unlike these, and the labor of love requisite to building these virtues, as habits to think, feel, and act in loving ways, follow suit. And this is, indeed, quite distinct from the requisites of just having sex, even incredibly orgasmic sex!

According to Alan Goldman (1977), sexual desire is just the desire for contact with another person's body and for the pleasure that such contact produces. There is thus no intrinsic purpose beyond the fulfillment of this desire. Thus, while traditional approaches to sex, such as that of Roger Scruton (1994), have anchored sexual desire in procreation as an essential purpose, for Goldman just having sex has no further purpose beyond the mere pleasure of physical contact. So, no breach of duty, no misuse of one's body, occurs when one has sex outside a committed, procreative relationship. Here, the morality of sex is one thing, and just having sex is another. Indeed, the analysis of the latter in terms of the former fails to capture the superb nature of a loving relationship that gives birth to sexual intimacy, with or without the added intention of bearing offspring in the act of making love.

Insofar as sexual desire is a desire for physical contact with someone else's body, it is primarily a mechanical activity. Rubbing, touching, caressing, kissing, sucking, biting, and, in general, the stimulation of the genitalia, whether in homo- or hetero-erotic encounters, are all mechanical in this sense. For they are all aimed primarily at mechanical stimulation or arousal. In just having sex, these physical activities have a self-regarding climax. Each partner uses the other to attain an organism.

Immanuel Kant (1930) keys into the symbiotic nature of just having sex. "Sexual love," he says, "makes of the loved person an Object of *appetite*; as soon as that appetite has been stilled, the person is cast aside as one casts away a lemon which has been sucked dry" (p. 163). However, for Kant, purely self-regarding sex becomes other-regarding when each partner begins to perceive the other as a person rather than as a mere object or thing. This, he says, can happen only in the context of a monogamous relationship of marriage when "under the one condition, that as the one person is acquired by the other as a thing, that same person also equally acquires the other reciprocally, and thus regains and reestablishes the rational *personality*." For, it is in this context that each partner contractually gives the other a right to their body. Such reciprocal sexual activity is, for Kant, possible only in the context of monogamous *marriage* where each sex partner gives the other a contractual right to the other's body. Such informed, mutual consent in a committed relationship is, indeed, a precursor to making love, and this is consistent with respect for one's personal autonomy or self-determination, which Kant, to his credit, emphasizes in his moral philosophy (Kant, 2004). However, there is much more to making love. For such mutuality is still based upon reciprocity of mechanical, self-interested arousal.

In contrast, in making love, you and I coalesce as one, for you and I are joined in a unity that is greater than either of us. This unity is not captured by "we" or "us" since "we" and "us" resolve into you and me, whereas the unity is indivisible. There is amalgamation without partition. "Erotic love begins with separateness and ends in oneness," speaks social psychologist Eric Fromm (1955, p. 34).

Still, philosophers of antiquity have pointed to a deeper, metaphysical interpretation of making love. For Aristotle (1941), true love is an extreme form of friendship where the two lovers are likened to occupying a "single soul" (bk. 9, ch. 8). While, for Plato (2012), when a true lover finds their soulmate, it is "the other half" of one soul that once inhabited heaven, split in half on earth, now in search of the (literal) other half; wherefore "the pair are lost in an amazement of love and friendship and intimacy, and one will not be out of the other's sight." And if asked if they would desire to be melded into one soul, there would not be one of them who "would deny or would not acknowledge that this meeting and melting into one another, this becoming one instead of two, was the very expression of his ancient need" (p. 74).

Metaphor, myth, or article of faith, such ancient accounts capture the cognitive–emotive tenor of this unity. For in making love, there is the surreal impression that your body is mine, and mine yours; that the sweet throbbing and titillations I am sensing are yours, and the ones you are sensing are mine. So that your past, present, and future—the childhood experiences shared; our hopes, *dreams*, and expectations—intertwine and coalesce with an ecstatic resonance that defies any breach in oneness.

This is not to suggest that all attempts at making love rise to the occasion, and that true love is perfect. Thus, a sleep-deprived lover, or one whose mind is elsewhere (a problem at work, an illness, hard times, a spat with one's beloved, or otherwise out of sorts), may strain lovemaking, and the rendezvous had better await another time. So, the lovers are tolerant and patient, but never perfectly so. After all, human beings and the material world they inhabit are imperfect.

Lovemaking is not hit or miss; it is infused with virtue, which is the product of habit, fortified through practice. Practice, however, will never make one perfect at making love; for the latter is always evolving, getting better and better, unbounded, and infinitely advancing toward its ultimate end—ecstatic, indivisible unity. The caress, ever so gentle, can be gentler, the subtlety of timing and the right words, uttered at precisely the right time, can be even more subtle, more poetic, more harmonic, and the perfume even sweeter. The benevolent gestures made during everyday encounters can be more benevolent; the thoughtful attempts to be there during the vicissitudes of life can be less distracted, more caring, and less self-interested.

Nor can a lover reside in a lovemaking space constantly. Martin Buber (1937) teaches the distinction between standing in either an "I–Thou" or "I–It" relation to another (Buber). In making love, I relate to you as I to Thou, not as I to It. When I say Thou to you, you are not merely an object or thing that I am using for this or that purpose, but instead, you are Thou, and I am Thou to you. This means that, to me, you are everything (and conversely) and "fill the heavens," for all else "lives in [your] light" (pt. 1, ch. 7). However, Buber admonishes that this unity cannot be permanent, as I must at some point begin to see you as an "It." For example, in touching each other's body, each does they know is most erotically felt by the other. So, there is a sort of delicate, momentary analysis and deliberate targeting of a body part. But, instantaneously, each becomes Thou again with comingling of not just body but soul. In making love, there is thus a virtually seamless reciprocity between

I–It and I–Thou. Erich Fromm confirms Buber's points. "In the act of loving, I am one with all, and yet I am myself, a unique, limited mortal human being. Indeed, out of the very polarity of separateness and union, love is born and reborn." (Fromm, 1955, p. 32).

As Fromm (1956) emphasizes, standing in the lovemaking relationship requires relinquishing control over one's lover. "I want the loved person to grow and unfold for his own sake, and in his own ways, and not for the purpose of serving me" (p. 26). Sexual unity proscribes dominating and being dominated. Lovemaking is stillborn when one attempts to humiliate, manipulate, or control the other. The uninitiated may confuse the latter with making love, whereas such maneuvers serve to bifurcate you from me as separate beings, not unify us. The consequence may be orgasmic sex, even very potent orgasmic sex, but not lovemaking.

The poetry of making love follows suit. It reflects and inspires unity, not self-interestedness. "I want to fuck you" and similar vulgar expressions of lust are devoid of the creativity that inspires lovemaking. Such expressions treat another as a mere thing "to be sucked dry" and "cast away" like Kant's proverbial lemon.

Contrast such vulgar expressions with that of Shakespeare's Portia in The Merchant of Venice: "And the other half—my own half, I'd call it—belongs to you too. If it's mine, then it's yours, and so I'm all yours." Such expressions invite unity, coalescence of two into one, in contrast to the language of just having sex, which divides and objectifies.

Of course, those profoundly important words, "I love you," may be spoken as foreplay to making love, or even during sexual experience. However, the speaker may really mean, "I am sexually attracted to you," and the recipient may understand it in this sense. Uttering these special words in this sense is not likely to conduce to lovemaking unless one is already *in* love and the seeds of lovemaking have already been sown. For two individuals already in love, these words tenderly uttered as an expression of the deep, heartfelt commitment to the other, can be a potent catalyst to lovemaking.

As such, the ability to make love tends to be the offspring to being in love. One dare not claim this is always the case, for there is no formal contradiction in making love without being *in* love. However, in this case, there would be tension between what transpires inside and outside the bedroom—on the one hand, the bond of unity, sexually, and the lack of intimacy in the overall relationship, on the other.

Such tension strains romantic love, as the latter tends to be in cognitive, emotional, and behavioral alignment. Like the performance of an intricate musical score by a full orchestra in which each instrument comes in at the right time, harmoniously blending into a coherent whole, romantic lovers are intimately keyed into one another's cognitive, emotional, and behavioral lives. "We both looked at each other, and I knew just what they were thinking," "I could have predicted they would react that way," "I knew what they were going through and didn't want to upset them with any unnecessary details." Indeed, the sexual dimension of romantic love is part of a broad spectrum of close interpersonal cognitive, behavioral, and emotional exchanges, including those surrounding the mundane issues of everyday life. This means that dysfunctional modes of relating outside the bedroom can disrupt the intimacy of what transpires inside it.

Six Impediments to Romantic Love

Many people spend a lifetime seeking romantic love and never attain it. "I just can't find someone with whom I'm compatible" "There's always something wrong with the people I meet"; "I am not willing to settle"; "No one likes me"; "I just can't seem to get it right"; "Things go well at first and then they fizzle out!"; "The sex is great but we just can't get along." Such excuses can be multiplied, *ad nauseam*, without getting one jot closer to identifying what has really gone wrong.

Unfortunately, many couples who pursue romantic love fail to realize that such love does not suddenly arise when the lights go out, or after wining and dining in an intimate setting. It is far more complex, and perhaps one of the most nuanced of interpersonal relationships. This may be partly due to the sexual aspect of the relationship. Indeed, it is understandable how just having orgasmic sex, with its incredibly high potential for physical satisfaction, can be thought the primary goal of a romantic relationship. Easy enough, it seems, to overlook the distinctive interpersonal aspects of this special relationship!

For the past several decades, I have worked with many individuals whose interpersonal relationships, from their sex lives to their careers, have suffered because of certain *impediments* consisting of very salient cognitive–behavioral habits—tendencies to think, feel, and act in self-defeating ways. While these habits are invariably the elephants in the room, those who repeatedly demonstrate them tend to be oblivious to them, or else discount their importance. As a result, these people repeat the same self-defeating things and then lament their inability to forge meaningful interpersonal relationships.

A constructive approach to overcoming such self-defeating habits is based on the ancient idea that one's character is composed largely of habits to act, think, and feel in certain ways, which are formed through practice. "Thus, in one word," says Aristotle (1941), "states of character arise out of like activities. This is why the activities we exhibit must be of a certain kind; it is because the states of character correspond to the differences between these" (bk. 2, ch. 1). In tune with Aristotle, the philosophical therapy developed in this book is based on the idea that there are certain "bad habits" that stifle romantic love.

According to this approach, overcoming such negative habits involves changing the way one acts, thinks, and feels when engaging in certain activities. For example, a person who is in a habit of complaining excessively can work on reframing situations by focusing on the more positive aspects of situations, and thereby refrain from complaining so much. In fact, there is abundant evidence that such cognitive-behavioral interventions can actually change dysfunctional neurological pathways in the human brain (Porto et al., 2009).

Now, there are six salient interpersonal dysfunctions or "unlovable habits" that often derail the prospects for romantic love for many couples. These problematic ways of relating do not address other possible factors such as sexual dysfunctions that have physiological etiologies. Nor do they include ones arising from mental disorders such as psychoses and personality disorders. It would therefore be an overgeneralization to suppose that all aborted attempts at romantic love are due to one or more of the impairments identified here. Each of these habits is identified in Table I.1.

Table I.1. Unlovable habits

Unlovable Habit (Impediment)	Description
Demanding perfection	I demand that I or my partner perform perfectly or near perfectly in bed, or make other demands on myself or my partner, which create considerable stress in our relationship.
Ego-obsessing	I generally expect my partner to do what pleases me. I think considerably less about what pleases my partner.
Self-damning	I often think of myself as inferior or not really worthy of my partner's respect.
Damning others	I often mock, say, or think negative things about my partner when they don't have an orgasm, is not good in bed, or otherwise messes up.
Exercising poor self-control	I tell myself that I can't control my emotions, take risks, stop thinking about bad things, or tolerate certain people or things.
Catastrophizing	I tend to think the worst by magnifying risks or oversimplifying reality, so things look worse than they probably are.

These six impediments often occur as *syndromes* where one of them leads to others. For example, because I demand that I perform perfectly in bed, I damn myself when I don't, and then tell myself I can't try anymore. Or I tell myself that I must be certain that our relationship will work before getting engaged, and, seeing that it's still not certain it will work, I tell myself that I can't take the risk.

The Virtues of Love

While cognitive–behavioral approaches to improving relationships usually seek to help people avoid self-defeating habits like the above ones, they do not typically provide aspirational goals or virtues to aim at. This is unfortunate, since romantic love is aspirational in character—it is itself an ideal or virtuous way of life. Accordingly, the approach developed here, based on Logic-Based Therapy, a form of philosophical counseling, provides counteracting virtues or ideals (Cohen, 2017). That is, for each of the above unlovable habits, there is a virtue that guides one in pursuit of an interpersonal relationship that fosters romantic love. Table I.2 displays these virtues paired to the unlovable habits that each counteracts.

As Aristotle (1941) astutely observed, such virtues as rational goals are "means" between extremes of excess and deficiency, that is, habits to pursue moderation in one's actions, emotions, and behavior (ch. 6, bk. 2). For example, empathy involves a point of moderation between the extremes of being too close and too far from a person's subjective world (Cohen, 2017). Avoiding these extremes in the context of an intimate relationship can present a challenge insofar as a lover's personal feelings may place a strain on distancing herself from the situation. "I can't believe you feel this way about me!" is an example of being too close. "I can understand how you feel turned off by how I have been treating you" is an example of proper distancing.

Importantly, it is unlikely that a lover can relate virtuously to his partner without being able to relate virtuously to others, as well. Thus, it is unlikely I can empathize with my lover if I cannot empathize with others. Moreover, virtuous treatment of some but not others would be inauthentic. As such, the cultivation of the virtues involves practicing them both *within and without the relationship*.

This means that the approach to romantic love taken in this book is a *systems* approach. This means that your relationship with your partner is viewed as part of a larger system of interpersonal relationships (family, friends, coworkers, etc.). As such, dysfunctional relationships, in one part of your system (say at work), can lead to problems elsewhere in the system, such as in your relationship with your

Table I.2. Unlovable habits and their counteracting virtues

Unlovable Habit (Impediment)	Counteracting Virtue	Description of Virtue
Ego-obsessing	Empathy	Transcending your own subjective universe to sense what others sense.
Self-damning	Self-respect	Unconditional self-acceptance based on a deep philosophical understanding of human worth and dignity.
Damning of others	Respect for others	Unconditional acceptance of the worth and dignity of other human beings.
Demanding perfection	Serenity	Reframing the world, or some aspect of it, by letting go of unrealistic demands that it be perfect.
Exercising poor self-control	Self-control	Exercising your willpower muscle to control what you do, how you feel, what you think, and your level of tolerance for others or for things you don't like or find difficult or challenging.
Catastrophizing	Courage	Confronting adversity without under- or overestimating the danger.
	Foresightedness	The ability to make predictions about the future that are probable relative to the facts as known.
	Objectivity	The ability to make judgments about people and the world that are unbiased and do not oversimplify reality.

partner, and conversely. Consequently, I give you cognitive–behavioral tools to address the six aforementioned impediments, as they arise in your relationship with your partner (inside and outside the bedroom), and in your relationships with other people too.

Further, as aspirations, the virtues can never be completely actualized. For example, one can always find new ways to express oneself authentically, and it is possible to backslide; for example, begin to lose yourself in a bandwagon of social conformity. Thus, the cultivation of virtue is a lifetime project. As Aristotle (1941) so eloquently admonished, "For one swallow does not make a summer, nor does one day; and so too one day, or a short time, does not make a man blessed and happy" (bk. 1, ch. 7).

Embracing a Love Philosophy

The rich history of philosophical ideas can itself provide guiding lights in the cultivation of virtue in a loving relationship. For example, Stoic philosophers such as Epictetus teach us not to try to control what is not in one's power to control (Epictetus, 2000). Thus, one who attempts to manipulate and control their partner's thoughts and emotions in attempting to build a loving relationship may defeat their own purposes. On the other hand, a partner who recognizes and accepts the limits of such control can find greater peace and serenity, both inside and outside their relationship.

So, the Stoic wisdom, of not attempting to control things not in your control, crystalizes in counsel on how to relate to your partner in the bedroom. For example, empirical research and clinical studies on female orgasm suggest that sexual perfectionists' attempt to control sexual intercourse, demanding that everything be perfect, leads to anxiety that stifles orgasm and overall performance (Stoeber & Harvey, 2016). Thus, Stoic wisdom admonishes sexual perfectionists to give up their self-defeating demand. This, in turn, involves "homework" assignments to practice overcoming this demand. Indeed, many sexual perfectionists demand perfection in other aspects of their relationships, so these assignments need not be limited to sexual activities (Cohen, 2019). In addition, such exercises like "rational-emotive imagery" allow aspiring romantic lovers to imagine themselves in situations in which they demand perfection, and to practice "letting go" based on Buddhist constructs of reality (Cohen, 2022).

A Five-Step Method for Making Constructive Change

So, philosophical wisdom can help aspiring romantic lovers strive for one of the most profoundly gratifying and life-affirming relationships known to humankind. This is no small contribution to human prosperity!

Each chapter of this book proceeds systematically according to a five-step process for making constructive interpersonal change toward enduring romantic love:

1. Recognizing a specific unlovable thinking syndrome as an impediment to enduring, romantic love,
2. Identifying a lovable virtue/s that counter this impediment,
3. Selecting personal philosophies that build this virtue/s,
4. Embracing the core philosophies, and
5. Applying your personal and core philosophies by practicing them.

In each chapter, one or more of the six forms of unlovable thinking mentioned earlier in this Introduction is examined. As you work through the chapters of this book, some impediments are likely to resonate more with you than others. For example, you might have realized that you tend to think of yourself as not being worthy of your partner's respect and that this has adversely affected your relationship. On the other hand, you may not believe that you engage in ego-obsession. So, in applying Step 1 of the above model, you are the one who will need to identify the specific impediments you want to focus on.

Please keep in mind that there is likely to be more than one impediment blocking your path to a long and prosperous love life. As mentioned, this is because impediments often form syndromes. This, in turn, means that you are likely to have more than one virtue to work on. For example, if you demand perfection in bed and then damn yourself when you don't achieve it (as inevitably you won't), then the loveable virtues you would focus on cultivating in Step 2 would be *self-respect* and *serenity*. The former counters self-damnation; and the latter, demanding perfection.

In this case, in Step 3, you would select philosophies, from among the ones provided, that resonate *with you*. For example, suppose you are deeply religious. To work on becoming more self-respecting, you might feel that a religious philosophy speaks best to you, such as the one that says that, as a human being, you are very special because you are a child of God. Reframing your self-worth, in these terms, might feel very empowering to you, so you might use this philosophy to work on overcoming your self-doubts. On the other hand, if you tend to be more secular, you might resonate more with Immanuel Kant's philosophy that counsels you to treat yourself as an *end in itself* and not as a *mere means*. This means that, to have or maintain your worth and dignity, you do not need to please your partner, perform well in bed, gain their approval, or otherwise fulfill some designated purpose. Instead, says Kant, you are a self-determining person ("end in itself"), not some mere object ("means") whose worth depends on the capacity to serve this or that purpose. So understood, Kant's philosophy can provide a way to accept your dignity and self-worth, without bringing in God.

Each chapter of this book provides an eclectic philosophy of love for building certain lovable virtues. These eclectic philosophies consist of a set of key philosophical ideas extracted from all the preceding, more specific philosophies presented. In Step 4, you should reflect on the key philosophical ideas for the virtues you want to work on, such as self-respect and serenity, and internalize them, that is, adopt them as your own. These key ideas should, at least for the most part, resonate with you. However, if there is any aspect that doesn't, you should not feel compelled to follow it.

Finally, in Step 5, please follow the guidelines constructed in each respective chapter to apply your personal and core philosophies. This is the section entitled "Applying the Eclectic Philosophy through Cognitive–Behavioral Practice." So, for example, to work on being more self-respecting in your relationship, you would avoid calling yourself derogatory terms such as "stupid" or "boring." Instead, sticking to rating your actions rather than yourself, as a person, you would focus on the things you do that you would like to change, like putting yourself down in front of others. In addition to the guidelines is a set of cognitive–behavioral exercises in each chapter that can provide further help in working on overcoming the given impediment and developing its respective lovable virtue. Finally, each chapter contains a brief video in which I talk to you about some of the main issues raised in the chapter.

I recommend sharing this book with your partner and working together, of possible. Being on the same page can itself create a synergy that proves efficacious in moving toward enduring, romantic love. This does not mean that you and your partner need to work on the same impediment if it is not equally an impediment for both of you. For example, you may need to work harder on self-respect than your partner, and your partner may need to worker harder on self-control than you do. Nevertheless, candidly sharing what each is working on and being open to constructive feedback from each other, in making progress toward the virtues in question, can be incredibly helpful. So, both you and your partner should, if possible, read this book, and work together toward constructive change.

What if your partner does not want to work through this book with you? This may be even more reason for you to work through it yourself! This is because, unless constructive changes are made somewhere in your system, no constructive changes are likely to occur anywhere else in your system. So, positive change in the way you relate to your partner can lead to constructive change in the way your partner (eventually) responds to you. Expect resistance, but improvement can occur if you disengage from the impediments blocking true love; pursue loveable virtues instead, guided by empowering philosophical ideas; be persistent; and, consequently, cease being your partner's codependent.

So, here, in this introduction, is the bird's eye view of the new philosophical therapy for enduring love and sexual intimacy developed in this book. It amalgamates the best of cognitive–behavioral approaches to overcoming some of the most self-destructive relationship habits. It does so by replacing them with positive, life-affirming goals in the form of virtues. Finally, it provides a set of cognitive–behavioral recommendations for achieving each of these virtues, based on the wisdom of the ages. The beauty of such a systematic approach to romantic love is surpassed only by the beauty of an enduring love, delicately intertwined with the ecstatic and ineffable unity of making love.

References

Aristotle. 1941. "Nicomachean Ethics." Trans. W. D. Ross. In *The Basic Works of Aristotle*, ed. by Richard McKeon, 930–1112. New York: Random House.
Buber, M. 1937. *I and Thou*. Trans. R. G. Smith, T.&T. Clark. Retrieved from https://archive.org/details/IAndThou_572/mode/2up.
Cohen, Elliot D. 2015, May 17. "How to be Empathetic: Find Out What You Can Do to Improve Your Relationships." *Psychology Today*. https://www.psychologytoday.com/us/blog/what-would-aristotle-do/201505/how-be-empathetic.
Cohen, Elliot D. 2017. *Logic-Based Therapy and Everyday Emotions: A Case-Based Approach*. Lanham, MD: Lexington Books.
Cohen, Elliot D. 2019, June 2. "Is Sexual Perfectionism Destroying Your Sex Life? Why Sexual Anxiety May Be Due to Perfectionism, And What You Can Do About It." *Psychology Today*.https://www.psychologytoday.com/us/blog/what-would-aristotle-do/201906/is-sexual-perfectionism-destroying-your-sex-life.
Cohen, Elliot D. 2022. *Cognitive Behavior Therapy for Those Who Say They Can't*. New York: Routledge.
Epictetus. 2000. *Enchiridion*. Trans. E. Carter. The Internet Classic Archive. http://classics.mit.edu/Epictetus/epicench.html.
Fromm, Erich. 1955. *The Sane Society*. New York: Henry Holt & Co.
Fromm, Erich. 1956. *The Art of Loving*. New York: Harper & Row.
Goldman, Alan. 1977. "Plain Sex." *Philosophy and Public Affairs*, 6(3), 267–287.
Kant, Immanuel. 1930. *Lectures on Ethics*. Trans. L. Infield. London: Methuen & Co. https://archive.org/stream/dli.ernet.3873/3873-Lectures%20On%20Ethics_djvu.txt.
Kant, Immanuel. 2004. *Fundamental Principles of The Metaphysics of Morals*. Trans. T. K. Abbott. Project Gutenberg E-book. https://www.gutenberg.org/files/5682/5682-h/5682-h.htm.
Plato. 2012. *Symposium*. Trans. Benjamin Jowett. Kindle Edition.
Plotinus. 1956. *Plotinus: The Enneads*, Trans. Stephen Mackenna. London: Faber & Faber, Ltd.
Porto, Patricia Ribeiro, Oliveira, Leticia, Mari, Jair, Volchan, Eliane, Figueira, Ivan, Ventura, Paula. 2009. "Does Cognitive Behavioral Therapy Change the Brain? A Systematic Review of Neuroimaging in Anxiety Disorders." *The Journal of Neuropsychiatry and Clinical Neurosciences*, 21(2): 114–125. https://doi.org/10.1176/jnp.2009.21.2.114.
Scruton, Roger. 1994. *Sexual Desire a Philosophical Investigation*. London: Bloomsbury Publishing.
Stoeber, Joachim & Harvey, Laura N. 2016. "Multidimensional Sexual Perfectionism and Female Sexual Function: A Longitudinal Investigation." *Archives of Sexual Behavior*, 45(8): 2003–2014. https://doi.org/10.1007/s10508-016-0721-7.

CHAPTER 1

BUILDING SERENITY IN ROMANTIC LOVE

> It must be obvious, from the start, that there is a contradiction in wanting to be perfectly secure in a universe whose very nature is momentariness and fluidity.
>
> —Alan Watts, *The Wisdom of Insecurity*

Romantic love is an ideal that is always in the process of becoming, that is, never fully actualized. It is therefore never perfect. Thus, *demanding* that it be perfect is self-defeating and creates needless stress for both partners.

Unfortunately, many aspiring lovers who demand perfection in their relationships find it difficult to let go of the idea that their relationships must be perfect; yet, they are clueless when things don't work out as expected. These disillusioned perfectionists may demand that both they and their partners perform perfectly in bed and upset themselves when they perceive sex to have fallen short of their demands. They may attempt to control their partners' lives, both inside and outside the bedroom, "making sure" everything works out according to plan. They may demand certainty about everyday decisions. As a result, they experience intense anxiety about the possibility of things going wrong in the future, and feel despondent or guilty when they do.

Notwithstanding, many perfectionists I have worked with have tended to wear their perfectionism as a badge of honor, proclaiming that their perfectionism is a good thing and even that we all have a responsibility to strive for excellence in our life pursuits. And, no doubt, they have a point. However, there is an important distinction between striving for excellence, including perfection, and *demanding* that one attain it. While striving for excellence makes good sense in the pursuit of romantic love, since the latter relationship is itself an ideal, *demanding* perfectionism makes no sense whatsoever. This is because, as emphasized here, romantic love is always in the process of becoming, and can never be perfect. Hence, the demanding perfectionist sabotages the relationship by demanding what is unrealistic.

Recognizing that Demanding Perfection is an Impediment

As impediments to sexual performance, demanding perfection manifests itself in terms of several self-defeating demands or "musts." These include the following:

- I must always come to orgasm, have perfect timing (not too early or too late), and (in males) have a sustained, hard erection; otherwise there's something terribly wrong with me.
- I must give my partner an orgasm, and always succeed in keeping them sexually satisfied.
- I must control everything before and during sex so that everything is perfect.
- My partner must do everything that I want them to do in bed (touch me in the right places, perform the sexual acts that I want, exactly as I want it, etc.); otherwise, they're no good in bed.
- My partner must give me sex whenever I am in the mood; otherwise, they're treating me unfairly.
- I must be certain (or near certain) that I won't mess up during sex (fail to have an orgasm, come to orgasm too soon, or experience sexual dysfunction).

These demands lead to anxiety before sex and during sex; produce guilt insofar as you blame yourself for transgressing what "must" be; or produce anger toward your partner when you perceive your partner to be at fault. Such emotional stress defeats the very goal of having orgasmic sex, let alone making love. In other words, these "musts" chill off the possibility of the enduring sexual intimacy emblematic of romantic love.

It is not idealism that has the chilling effect. Aspiring for perfectionism in the bedroom—aspiring to attain that indescribable ecstasy of two individuals perfectly coalescing into one, letting go of all negative judgments, relinquishing control, ceasing to scrutinize and critique, surrendering rather than protecting oneself—is precisely the form of perfectionism needed to make love. For, in this attitude there is no demand for perfection, but rather the vision of the blissful encounter, the thrust toward its pursuit with exuberance and excitement, not anxiety, guilt, or anger.

But this is only the tip of the iceberg! It is important to recognize that perfectionism exists on a broad spectrum. That is, perfectionists tend to make perfectionistic demands about many activities in their lives, from sexual relations to many other aspects of their lives—school, work, friendship, and other interpersonal relations. This means that overcoming perfectionism in building a romantic relationship includes working on the same problem as it arises in other life contexts. For example, overcoming perfectionist demands about school or work can help with giving up making such demands in intimate relationships, including sexually.

This is because demanding sexual perfection is typically a manifestation of a more general habit of thinking, feeling, and acting in certain ways. Thus, the "musts" listed above may be considered corollaries of higher-order "musts" or demands in one's repertoire of self-imposed demands:

- I must be perfect (at least) at the things that are important to me.
- Others must never treat me unfairly.
- I must always be in control.
- I must always get the approval of others.
- I must be certain that bad things won't happen.
- Others must do what I want.

Such generic "musts," in turn, direct behavioral and emotional responses. Thus, people who demand perfection in their performance, such as at work or school-related activities, tend to be self-loathing when they fail to perform up to par. They may withdraw socially when they mess up or avoid challenging activities altogether.

People who demand that others treat them fairly tend to become angry when they perceive others to have treated them unfairly, and they may respond aggressively toward them.

Many who demand the approval of others are conformists who may even do things they know are wrong just to fit in or get accepted. Such individuals may have a difficult time accepting criticism because they take it as a sign of disapproval and may become self-defensive or pouty.

People who demand control tend to violate the autonomy of others in attempting to make sure they are on top of things. They tend to experience intense, ongoing anxiety when embarking on activities, even ones that are supposed to be recreational or enjoyable.

People who demand certainty about things tend to shy away from doing things that involve risks. When they do decide to engage in activities, they tend to exaggerate the bad things that could happen and worry and ruminate about even extremely remote possibilities.

People who demand that others do what they want, tend to be difficult to get along with because it's their way or the (proverbially) highway. They tend to be stubborn and uncooperative and often arouse animosity from others in social situations.

Clearly, demanding perfectionists, like the ones mentioned above, are not likely to experience enduring romantic love and sexual intimacy so long as they maintain such self-stultifying habits!

Demanding Perfection in the Bedroom

In this video, I discuss these types of perfectionism and what they can mean inside (and outside) the bedroom. I suggest viewing it, before proceeding with the rest of this chapter!

https://youtu.be/49TBp48G7zE

Identifying serenity as a counter to demanding perfection

The positive news is that it is possible to give up these habits through the pursuit of serenity. Indeed, striving for serenity in one's life is incompatible with demanding perfection because the latter makes an impossible demand, and one can be anything but serene when one is hell-bent on achieving what is not achievable!

The pursuit of serenity involves a reframing of the world in more realistic terms. This does not mean foreclosing one's fondest hopes and dreams. On the contrary, it involves perceiving the imperfections of reality as exciting challenges to overcome in aspiring toward such goals. It is an attitude of growth, in which one's mistakes are viewed as lessons to use in the pursuit of one's goals. It views risks as part of this inherent excitement, where opening one door leads to the discovery of others, some of which may never have been conceived prior. Thus, one may accidentally discover a new talent or pleasant activity through a willingness to take risks. This, in turn, may open up other opportunities. "I never thought that, in taking that first art course, I would end up becoming an accomplished artist with works displayed in an art gallery!"

Serenity means that one has attained a measure of peace of mind, unperturbed about many of the inevitable negative things that happen; being able to see the larger picture, in which it becomes evident that, yesterday's fender bender is not the end of the world. It is to appreciate a small act of kindness conferred by a stranger, or that look in your partner's eyes when you tell her how much you love her.

Serenity is a habit or disposition to put things into perspective, neither overreacting nor underreacting to the situation at hand. This is a point of moderation between excessive emotions; extreme behavioral responses; and over-reactive value assessments—"This is horrible" and "This is wonderful"—when the reality is somewhere between.

As a habit, serenity does not preclude occasional self-disturbing, self-defeating emotions, cognitions, and behavior. This is because habits are tendencies, which means that they admit of occasional lapses. So, a couple romantically in love may interact irrationally on occasion (for example, quarrel), but this does not mean that the two lovers are not serene. The latter would be true only if the tendency toward serenity were replaced with a self-disturbing, self-defeating *tendency*.

Serenity is not a sufficient condition of romantic love, although it is a necessary one. Thus, a serene couple may be good friends, and enjoy a Platonic relationship. Such a relationship may be quite suitable for some; however, it is clearly not the same thing as being romantically in love. On the other hand, a couple is not going to cultivate romantic love insofar as one or both partners is a demanding perfectionist, and, consequently, creates a climate of emotional stress.

Again, it is unlikely that an individual is going to find serenity in his relationship (including inside the bedroom) when he or she demands perfection outside the relationship. Indeed, when a person has acquired a habit of demanding perfection, it is unlikely this person can turn off this habit *inside* the relationship. The more likely consequence is that the person will create a climate of emotional stress within the relationship as well.

So how can a couple pursue serenity in their lives, inside *and* outside of their relationship?

Philosophies that Build Serenity

Fortunately, some of the greatest minds of antiquity have had insights that bear directly on the above question. The philosophies discussed below, while not the only ones that could be brought to bear on serenity, can collectively address the various types of demanding perfection identified in this chapter and provide you with constructive guides for overcoming them in pursuit of romantic love.

Everything, including your partner, is perfectly imperfect

Lao Tzu (2009), the founder of the ancient Chinese philosophy of Taoism, states in his *Tau Te Ching*, "True perfection seems imperfect, yet it is perfectly itself [...]" (45). The point is that one cannot strive for perfection without also embracing imperfection at the same time because it is an unavoidable part of reality. After all, one's imperfections are inherent features of what makes one an individual as distinct from other individuals.

In this individuality inheres perfection, so that one is "perfectly imperfect"! As such, couples pursuing romantic love may come to embrace their partners' imperfections as aspects of the individuals they love. This does not mean that such couples cannot help each other to do better. It rather means that such improvements will themselves include imperfections that further individualize the beloved. Accordingly, any demand to eliminate imperfection from the other would prove self-defeating.

For one who demands perfection *of others*, Lao Tzu might therefore advise making a list of those imperfections of your partner that uniquely qualifies the person. These can include quirks and idiosyncrasies. For example, the person may have a bad sense of direction, cries at movies, has severe myopia, and becomes giddy after just one glass of wine. There may be more pervasive "imperfections," such as being wheelchair-bound while refusing to be held back by it, which make the person especially laudable, indeed courageous. In general, such distinctive characteristics may make the person lovable, endearing, virtuous, or otherwise special. One can thus begin to transcend the false dichotomy of perfection versus imperfection by ceasing to focus on the flaws in your partner and to perceive this person more holistically.

There is a "Yin in every Yang," that is, a unity of opposites so that what one might find to be positive is only understood in terms of its negative, and conversely (Sun, 2009). This idea of unity is a wonderful basis for making love, for all elements of distinction, positive and negative, are therein lost in an ecstatic unity of two as one.

Pain is inevitable, suffering is not

The founder of Buddhism also speaks of unity and admonishes against getting absorbed in oneself. For Buddha, the belief in a permanent self is itself illusory because everything, including consciousness, is in a constant state of change (Goldhill, 2015). "All is impermanence" ("anicca").

This has important implications for demanding perfectionists who demand that others do what they want; for if the self is illusory, self-centeredness is misguided. Thus, the more that self-absorbed perfectionists demand that the world conform to their desires, the more frustrated they become; for they can never satisfy their perfectionist demands. For Buddha, the way out of this trap is to replace self-interestedness with selflessness, as exercised in showing compassion for others. In so doing, one can free oneself of the oppression of constantly attempting to feed an ego that can never be perfectly satisfied, for as soon as the self gets what it wants, it changes its desires and wants something else, and so on *ad nauseam*.

The Buddha's "First Noble Truth" speaks directly to the danger of demanding what one cannot have (Cohen, 2007):

> Now this is the noble truth of pain: birth is painful, old age is painful, sickness is painful, death is painful; sorrow, lamentation, dejection, and despair are painful. Contact with unpleasant things is painful. In short, the five groups of grasping [the body, feelings, ideas, volitions, and conscious awareness] are painful (p. 69).

Hence, in demanding that such things not happen, one creates suffering for oneself and one's loved ones; for while the pain is inevitable, the suffering produced when one demands what is impossible, is avoidable. Serenity is therefore possible when one stops "grasping" for perfection and accepts that reality is imperfect. For the couple in search of romantic love, this also means relinquishing making self-centered demands on each other and instead striving for selfless compassion for one another. Such compassion builds love inside and outside the bedroom. Two who are romantically in love see each other as loci of intrinsic worth, not as instruments for satisfying individual desires. In sexual activity, the latter possessiveness only destroys the prospect of the unity essential to making love.

Unfortunately, those who focus on the pleasures they may attain in the future, or the pains they have endured in the past, lose sight of the here and now, which is where compassionate sharing occurs and serenity is practiced. Living in the future or the past can breed anxiety in one case and despondence in the other. For prospective romantic lovers, it is therefore necessary to direct attention to the here and now. Lamenting the past or stressing about future possibilities are two ways to scuttle the opportunity to find serenity in the here and now.

Bracketing the painful thoughts that come with demanding perfection can be practiced through *mindfulness meditation*. This involves focusing on a pleasant object or one's breathing, in the here and now, gently pushing intrusive negative thoughts away. Many people have found such meditative practice useful for reducing emotional stress. For aspiring romantic lovers, this may be a useful way to learn to focus on the present. In this way, you can avoid allowing your mind to be carried off course, losing the opportunity to share intimate moments. (See the featured exercise in this chapter on mindfulness meditation.)

You cannot control others, including your partner

The ancient Greek Stoic philosopher, Epictetus, arrives at a similar conclusion by distinguishing between what is in one's power to control and what is not. In his *Enchiridion* (2009), he eloquently states:

> Things in our control are opinion, pursuit, desire, aversion, and, in a word, whatever are our own actions. Things not in our control are body, property, reputation, command, and, in one word, whatever are not our own actions. The things in our control are by nature free, unrestrained, unhindered; but those not in our control are weak, slavish, restrained, belonging to others. Remember, then, that if you suppose that things which are slavish by nature are also free, and that what belongs to others is your own, then you will be hindered. You will lament, you will be disturbed, and you will find fault both

with gods and men. But if you suppose only things to be your own that are really yours, and what belongs to others really does belong to others, then no one will ever compel you or restrain you (ch. 1).

Hence, sticking to the control of your actions, including your own opinions, pursuits, desires, and aversions, you can eliminate the primary way you disturb yourself. No one can rationally fault a person for the pursuit of perfection, so long as the person gives up the demand for it. For, it is in your power to pursue perfection, but it is not in your power to attain it.

On the other hand, it is not in your power to control the actions of others, including the approval of your partner. As such, in demanding that you do so, you merely place your ability to relax and enjoy life at the mercy of the whims, moods, dispositions, and whatever else might move others to act.

Inasmuch as each partner is a free agent who sticks to exercising their own freedom, rather than attempting to stifle the freedom of the other, one can enjoy one's own free agency without the encumbrance of attempting to control that of another. Such mutual tolerance for autonomy is key to the serenity of a couple seeking romantic love.

In sexual activity, you cannot control all; for you are a fallible human. Thus, giving yourself permission to be fallible is not only reasonable but also it can save you from the abyss of self-defeating performance anxiety. Likewise, attempting to control your partner, for example, by manipulating the placement of your partner's hands, may help to increase the orgasm of the one who does the manipulating; but so too can self-stimulation. While just having sex and masturbation involve mechanical manipulation, making love is *sui generis*. The latter is never forced or exacted. The moment you try is the moment you lose the opportunity to make love.

The physical is but an imperfect copy of the ideal

However, even in its freest state, making love does not make gods of mere mortal beings. For, as the ancient Greek philosopher, Plato, would admonish, it will never lose the taint of its earthly origin.

According to Plato, the material world of space and time, including the human body, is a world of imperfect things that come into existence and go out of existence. Our bodies grow old and deteriorate. At their very best, they are imperfect. A beautiful body wrinkles with age, and any attempt to salvage it (through cosmetic surgery, for example) eventually meets with defeat.

However, according to Plato, physical objects are the incarnations of ideal or perfect Forms that they "participate" in. Thus, while a beautiful body will eventually wither and die, the Form of Beauty will remain unchanged, for eternity. Likewise, while there may be individual acts of injustice on Earth, the Form of Justice remains forever unchanged. For such objective realities enjoy an independent status outside of time and space.

In the physical universe, we have only imperfect copies of such Ideals, says Plato. Thus, no human being can be perfectly beautiful, good, truthful, and so forth. For like the reflection of a flower in a pond, which is an imperfect copy of the physical flower, the physical human being is fated to be imperfect (Plato, 2000).

So, in this view, there is a sort of category mistake a potential romantic lover can make; namely, confusing ideality with materiality. One can surely strive to "participate" more and more in the ideal, admonishes Plato, but such participation will never *be* ideal. So, given the existence of objective Forms of Truth, Goodness, and Beauty, it is futile to demand them in the material world.

Yet, how often do couples scrutinize their own bodies and those of their partners, lamenting even a minor blemish. Such preoccupation with bodily imperfection loses the forest for the trees. News flash: the human body is imperfect! In Plato's view, serenity requires giving up this demand for a perfect body.

It likewise requires giving up the *demand* for Fairness. Again, justice and fairness on Earth are administered imperfectly. Thus, no couple can be rationally expected to always treat each other fairly. But they can indeed realize their iniquities, apologize for them, and pursue (the ideal of) Justice in relation to their partners and everyone else here on earth, albeit without demanding they attain it!

Perfection is no more real than imperfection

However, one need not believe such objective Forms exist to reach similar conclusions. According to French contemporary philosopher, Jacque Derrida, "oppositional hierarchies," such as Plato's distinction between perfection and imperfection, can be "deconstructed." The idea here is that such a hierarchy can be reversed so that, instead of perfection being prior to imperfection, the latter can be tagged as prior. So that imperfection is the source of perfection since we could never even conceive of the latter without the former. But once you see that, the same logic that leads you to think perfection is the original term, can be reversed, you can also see that the whole business of creating such an oppositional hierarchy, in the first place, is boloney and should therefore be discarded.

For couples seeking romantic love, this means giving up the self-defeating demand for perfection since you might as well demand *im*perfection, which is equally as absurd. This, in turn, can free you to strive for romantic love without the pretense that it must be perfect to be "real."

So, from Derrida's perspective, freedom is a precondition of love. Deconstruction clears the path to this freedom, which is the ability to navigate life without the encumbrance of an oppositional hierarchy circumscribing the nature and limits of one's love for another.

According to Derrida, one such barrier to freedom is the idea that you must love "who" a person is, not "what" the person is. For example, people love others for the way they look tenderly into their lovers' eyes; the way they kiss; the tone of their voice; the way they smile; and their warm embrace; and, yes, even their idiosyncratic ways. Here, there is a deconstruction of the oppositional hierarchy of the who of the person as "an absolute singularity" and "the ways" of the person, whereby the hierarchy is reversed from loving the person *as such* to love *the ways* of the person.

However, there is a pitfall to avoid, namely, degrading others for their *negative* ways. This is a fallacy to be considered later, that of damning the *doer* rather than the deed. This is exactly what Derrida would denounce.

Identifying Some Core Philosophical Aspects of Serenity

As you can see, a philosophical approach to serenity of love and lovemaking is multipronged, drawing from diverse philosophical perspectives. Some of these perspectives may resonate better than others for certain love seekers since the personal worldviews of people often vary. So, "different (philosophical) strokes for different folks." Force-feeding a philosophy is as counterproductive to the promotion of romantic love as attempting to control your partner's sexual predilections.

For example, not everyone would accept Plato's idea that there is an ideal world from which physical things are copied; and not everyone would be inclined toward a perspective, such as that found in Buddhism and Taoism, that there is just one reality. Similarly, not everyone would agree with Buddhists that the self is illusory; and not all would agree that you cannot love "who" a person is, as well as "what" they are. Nevertheless, there are elements that can be extracted from the approaches discussed in this chapter, that appear to be germane to everyone's pursuit of romantic love. These aspects include, but are not limited to the following:

- Seeing your partner (as well as others) as a distinct individual, identifiable at least in part by his "imperfections";
- Having compassion for your partner as well as others;
- Not trying to control what is outside your control such as the actions of others, including the approval of others;
- Viewing yourself as fallible by virtue of being human, whose performance in bed as elsewhere may not always be stellar;
- Respecting the autonomy of your partner, sexually as well as outside the bedroom, instead of attempting to manipulate them;
- Not focusing on negative aspects of your partner, inside and outside the bedroom;
- Not being preoccupied with your own body or that of your partner;
- Seeing the intrinsic worth and dignity of your partner, instead of seeing this person merely as a vehicle for satisfying your own desires;
- Seeking unity in the pursuit of romantic love, rather than divisiveness;
- Recognizing the right of others to own their subjective perspectives even if they disagree with your own;
- Loving the ways of a person, not just who they are;
- Accepting your freedom to love and be loved; and
- Not living in the future or the past at the expense of the present.

These are arguably among the most fundamental aspects of serenity in romantic love no matter what individual philosophical conceptions you choose to embrace.

Applying the Eclectic Philosophy Through Cognitive-Behavioral Practice

Each of the above core elements of serenity requires practice, for it is not enough to accept it. As Aristotle (1941) makes clear, acquiring a virtue does not occur by merely reading a book. In the case of serenity, you will need to work cognitively and behaviorally to overcome your demanding perfectionism. Practice does not make perfect, but it is requisite to profound constructive change. You can work toward this goal by doing the cognitive-behavioral exercises and applying the guidelines I have provided for building serenity in your everyday life:

EXERCISE 1

Mindfulness Meditation: A Highly Effective Way to Work on Serenity

There have been many studies that show that mindfulness meditation can be useful for relieving emotional stress, including anxiety, which undermines serenity or peace of mind (American Psychological Association, 2019). One mindfulness program that I would highly recommend is that based on the program created by John Kabat-Zinn, which is offered online, free of charge (Palouse Mindfulness, n.d.). Here is the link: https://palousemindfulness.com/.

EXERCISE 2

Being Your Authentic Self

This activity is a version of what is known as a "shame-attacking exercise." (See also the first featured exercise in Chapter 3.) Its goal is to help increase authenticity by overcoming the perfectionistic demand for approval.

1. Practice letting go of the demand for approval of others. You can do this by doing or saying something that you think would be an authentic expression of your values. This should be something that you have not done before because you think others would judge you negatively. For example, perhaps you have a certain view about a social issue that you have avoided expressing because others such as your friends, family, or your partner would disagree with you. Then, when others disagree with you, use a philosophy from this chapter (or from elsewhere in this book) to accept yourself regardless of what others may be thinking about you. For example, consider the Stoic admonition to give up trying to control what is not in your power to control such as other people's thoughts and feelings. Reflect on how you feel about having been your authentic self.
2. Practice this activity, inside and outside the bedroom. For example, consider whether you are being your authentic self, sexually, or if you are simply doing, in bed, what is expected of you. If the latter, then a candid discussion with your partner about increasing your sexual freedom may prove helpful in making future constructive changes.

Guidelines for building serenity

- Write down as many of the idiosyncratic attributes ("quirks") of your partner that make them the unique person you are attracted to. This can help to reinforce the things about the person you love.
- Try not to control the outcomes of activities, including sex. Remember, you can't control your partner, and sex is a product of both of you.
- Practice giving yourself permission to be a fallible human being in bed as elsewhere. "So, I messed up. That's because I'm only human, and therefore imperfect just like all other humans."
- Speak to your partner, candidly, about your feelings, rather than being afraid to be negatively judged. (See also the second featured activity in this chapter.)
- Try out rational-emotive imagery to work on control issues. For example, imagine not having an orgasm during sex, and then, while imagining that this happened, cognitively work through your catastrophic thinking. "Okay, so what? Is it terrible, horrible, and awful, like being boiled alive in a vat of oil? Where is it written that I must always have an orgasm? If not having an orgasm makes me a failure, then all or most of us would be failures because this happens to everyone, or at least most people. If someone else I cared about told me they didn't have an orgasm, I wouldn't be down on them, so where is this double standard coming from?" (For more on catastrophic thinking, see Chapter 5.)

These cognitive–behavioral activities, including the ones featured here, can help you to cultivate a habit of serenity. It is not enough to pay lip service to the core philosophical elements of serenity (merely agreeing that you should work on them) while repeating the same self-destructive demands for perfection.

In fact, the various forms of demanding perfection discussed in this chapter undergird all or most of the impediments to romantic love discussed in subsequent chapters. For example, the refusal to acknowledge the rights of others to their beliefs, values, and desires derives from the perfectionistic demand that others agree with, or share your own subjective perspectives, or preferences.

The latter impediment, in turn, has a *further* virtue that counteracts or corrects it, namely *empathy*. By being empathetic with your partner, and seeing things from her subjective point of view, you will be less inclined to demand your way or the highway. As such, in romantic love, the virtues tend to be interdependent and mutually supportive. Accordingly, Chapter 2 will examine the latter virtue as a counteractive to self-obsessiveness, in relation to romantic love.

References

American Psychological Association. 2019, October 30. "Mindfulness Meditation: A Research-Proven Way to Reduce Stress." *Psychology Topics.* https://www.apa.org/topics/mindfulness/meditation.

Aristotle. 1941. Nicomachean Ethics. Trans. W. D. Ross. In *The Basic Works of Aristotle*, ed. by Richard McKeon, 930–1112. New York: Random House.

Cohen, Elliot D. 2007. *The New Rational Therapy*. Ithaca, NY: Prometheus Books.

Epictetus. 2009. *Enchiridion*. Trans. E. Carter. The Internet Classic Archive. http://classics.mit.edu/Epictetus/epicench.html.

Lao, Tzu. 2009. *Tao Te Ching*. New York: Harper Collins.

Plato. 2000. *The Republic*. Trans. B. Jowett. Internet Classics Archive. http://classics.mit.edu/Plato/republic.mb.txt.

Palouse Mindfulness. n.d. "Online Mindfulness-Based Stress Reduction (MBSR)." www.palousemindfulness.com.

Goldhill, Olivia. 2015. "Neuroscience Backs Up the Buddhist Belief that "The Self" Isn't Constant, but Ever-Changing." *Quartz*. https://qz.com/506229/neuroscience-backs-up-the-buddhist-belief-that-the-self-isnt-constant-but-ever-changing.

Sun, Key. 2009. "Using Taoist Principle of The Unity of Opposites to Explain Conflict and Peace." *The Humanistic Psychologist*, 37: 271–286. https://www.psychologytoday.com/sites/default/files/attachments/35629/using-taoist-principle-the-unity-opposites.pdf.

CHAPTER 2

BUILDING INTIMACY THROUGH EMPATHY IN ROMANTIC LOVE

> Focused on me at all times, you will overcome all obstructions; but if you persist in clinging to the I-sense, then you are lost.
>
> —*Bhagavad Gita*

Recognizing Ego-Obsessiveness as an Impediment

In true love, each partner brings something special to the loving relationship, and it is not possible to dictate the terms of this specialness. Unfortunately, if you demand that your partner conforms to your values, desires, and preferences, without reciprocal consideration of your partner's views, then your attempt at forging romantic love is not likely to succeed. This applies both inside as well as outside the bedroom!

Such a skewed relationship may exist on a continuum, where you may make some concessions but largely set the standards of what is acceptable and unacceptable within the relationship. At the extreme, you attempt to turn your partner into a servant who exists to serve you. You possess this person as though they were an object to be used to satisfy your desires and you reject them when they disagree or otherwise fail to conform to your demands.

Of course, we all interpret reality through our own subjective lenses. I cannot literally step outside my mind to experience reality in quite the way you do, and conversely. So, it is understandable how you may see things differently than I do, and I you. However, realizing that this is the case can be a first step in building a respectful rapport with your partner.

In ego-obsession, this does not happen. Rather, the ego-centered partner sets themselves up as a sort of reality guru who determines by fiat what is true or false, good or bad, right or wrong. This is the opposite of how we ordinarily think of truth and falsehood. Long ago, Aristotle (2000) succinctly summed up the everyday conception of truth and falsehood. He stated, "To say of what is that it is not, or of what is not that it is, is false, while to say of what is that it is, and of what is not that it is not, is true" (Bk. 4, Pt. 7). So, people's beliefs are true when they correspond to reality, and false when they do not. In contrast, the ego-obsessive individual tends to suppose that something is true when it corresponds to their beliefs, and false when it does not. From the ego-obsessive individual's perspective, reality does not determine the truth or falsity of their beliefs. Instead, *their beliefs* determine reality! So, if you wonder why attempts to reason with an ego-obsessive individual rarely, if ever, convince them that they are wrong, it is because the very concept of their being wrong is not possible from this person's epistemic perspective!

Does this sound like your partner? Does it sound anything like you? If so, there is wanting a chief ingredient of the romantic encounter, namely respect for the other's perspective. This involves a coalescence of values, the sharing of lived experience, the intermingling or interplay, and delicate acceptance of each other's values in a majesty of empathic resonance.

Identifying Empathy as a Counter to Ego-Obsessiveness

The good news is that empathy can be cultivated or improved by working on it. This does not necessarily mean that everyone has equal potential for empathy. But it does mean that we are all capable of making constructive changes in the way we meet and engage with one's partner's subjective world. Remember, it is unrealistic, and thus self-defeating to demand perfection in romance, and this clearly applies with respect to improving one's powers of empathy.

Like all other virtues, empathy is a habit that can improve with practice. To be an empathetic person does not mean that you *always* have empathy for others, for example, for certain individuals, whom you may not like, who are suffering or going through hard times. Rather, it means that you *tend* to have empathy for the plights of others.

According to renowned psychologist and creator of "Person-Centered Therapy," Carl Rogers (1974), there are several aspects of empathy. Having empathy means:

1. Entering the private perceptual world of the other and becoming thoroughly at home in it.
2. Being sensitive, moment to moment, to the changing felt meanings that flow in this other person; to the fear or rage or tenderness or confusion or whatever that they are experiencing.

3. Temporarily living in his life, moving about in it delicately, without making judgments, sensing meanings of which he is scarcely aware but not trying to uncover feelings of which he is totally unaware since this would be too threatening.
4. Communicating your sensing of his world as you look with fresh and unfrightened eyes at elements of which he is fearful.
5. Frequently checking with him as to the accuracy of your sensing and being guided by his responses.
6. You are a confident companion to him in his world. By pointing to the possible meanings in the flow of his experiencing, you help him to focus on this useful type of referent; to experience his meanings more fully and to move forward in his or her experiencing.

Having empathy in the context of romantic love thus means being able to resonate with the subjective world of your partner when they are experiencing negative feelings as well as positive ones. So, you share in the excitement over the good news your partner receives, as well as saddened by the bad news. In stepping into this shared emotional space, you feel a sense of belonging, not so much like a visitor who comes for a particular purpose, but rather like one who lives in this space. Of course, this is a metaphor, and you are not literally residing in this space, however you *feel as though* you do. This feeling is a function of parts of the human brain that are active, especially the part of the cerebral cortex called the insular cortex (Mount Sinai Medical Center, 2012).

This resonance is not an occasional thing in a loving relationship. It is a continuously reoccurring phenomenon in which you key into the fluctuating feelings arising from the stream of ideas that flow through your partner's conscious mind. You know what they are thinking, what these thoughts signify or mean to them, and how they are impacting how they feel. So, you know how disappointed your partner is about hearing the news that they did not get that job they wanted so badly; and you sense that sadness that envelops them. Thus, there is an intertwining of cognition (thought) and affect (feeling); not just a burst of feeling out of the blue, or a cold thought as a matter of fact, but instead a comingling of both. Indeed, the more you know about the events in your partner's life (for example, that they have been waiting for several years for this job to come along), the more you are able to empathically resonate with what your partner is going through. Thus, empathetic partners are communicative and disclosing to one another.

Nor is empathy unilateral in romantic love. Rather, there is a dynamic relationship whereby your empathetic regard for me synergizes my empathy for you, and conversely. It is not just about me, and how you can feel my pain. There is reciprocity, so that *we feel each other's pain (or joy)*. Empathy in the context of attempting to forge a romantic relationship with an ego-obsessive individual is thus a lonely universe to occupy. You are alone with your partner's feelings, and no one is living with you in your emotional quarters. This is hardly the breeding ground for enduring love, whether inside or outside the bedroom!

Where empathy is mutually attuned, in bed, your feelings of ecstasy feel like mine, and mine like yours. With every pulsation of your body, mine pulsates in calibration and the wall separating our corporeal titillations dissolves in a unified gestalt of shared experience. On occasions where sexual interchange does not lead to climax, there is no negative judgment, mockery, or other sign of rejection, which is emblematic of ego-obsession. Indeed, empathetic understanding is *non*judgmental. As soon as I begin to analyze your performance, and you analyze mine, amidst emotional sharing, the capacity to empathize evaporates and the residue of hard feelings takes its place. So maybe I am feeling like I let you down by my performance. You immediately sense my insecurity and embrace me tenderly to relieve my self-doubt. I, in turn, sense your tenderness and its meaning of unconditional acceptance. For I am not a machine that has just malfunctioned; I am your lover and your friend, the one you hold dear. And I am comforted. That's how empathy works, synergistically!

In the intercourse of daily life, outside the bedroom, empathy is marked by reflective listening and helping your partner to reframe in constructive ways problems of living that create anxiety, depression, anger, guilt, or other destructive emotions. I am not your personal therapist, and you are not mine, so the loss of objectivity on either of our parts is understandable, especially when the problem affects us both. But your tendency and mine to enter each's respective subjective worlds and resonate with its felt meanings make possible an alliance in addressing the vicissitudes of life.

I know how I felt when I was in similar circumstances, so I rely on my experience in putting myself in my partner's place. So, how did I feel when my best friend betrayed me? I recall the anger fluctuating with deep sadness, the hollow feeling in my chest, and the sleepless nights I spent trying to grapple with the issue. These feelings inform my own perception of what my partner might be going through in a similar situation. Yet, I try my level best not to let any unfinished business of my own taint my ability to sense my partner's felt meanings. This is not an occasion for the blind to lead the blind, but instead an opportunity to pool cognitive–emotive–behavioral resources to address the problem at hand. Importantly, my partner feels my commitment and allegiance, that they are not alone.

I do not merely assume that I am sensing my partner's felt meanings because mine might not accurately depict theirs. So, I frequently check with them about their accuracy.

> I really shared so much with my best friend, and now what we had is just gone.
> So, you feel *abandoned* by your best friend?

Here, you key into your partner's feelings by *reflecting back*, in an insightful way, what they have disclosed to you. Now, if your partner were to deny that they felt abandoned, then the exchange might have continued along these lines:

> No, not abandoned, I just didn't think they were capable of such a thing!
> So, you feel let down by them, that you trusted them with so much and they were not even worthy of this trust?
> Yes, exactly, like I never should have trusted them in the first place. Boy, what a mistake!

This is not merely a mechanical parroting back of what your partner has revealed to you; instead, it facilitates your partner's deeper understanding of their own felt meanings in a way that only someone who was truly immersed in their partner's subjective world could accomplish. Such subjective sharing of each other's subjective worlds is, quite obviously, not possible if you are focused only or primarily on how *you* are feeling. As a result, you defeat your own purposes by depriving yourself of the incredible happiness you could attain through romantic love.

Empathy in Making Love

In this video, I discuss the nature of empathy and its place in making love.

https://youtu.be/qoquTBUPtTE

Philosophies that Build Empathy

Romantic love assumes equal, autonomous partners, neither dominating the other

In her classic work, *The Second Sex*, first published in 1949, philosopher Simone de Beauvoir (2010) eloquently exposes the hypocrisy inherent in a system of "romantic love" in which the man dominates and possesses the woman as a possession at his disposal. Sadly, fast-forwarding to contemporary times, many relationships, both gay and straight, bear the same mark of unilateral domination. According to de Beauvoir, what is missing in such a relationship is reciprocity, in which each recognizes the other as an autonomous human being. She states,

> The fact of being a human being is infinitely more important than all the singularities that distinguish human beings [...] The same drama of flesh and spirit, and of finitude and transcendence, plays itself out in both sexes; both are eaten away by time, stalked by death, they have the same essential need of the other; and they can take the same glory from their freedom; if they knew how to savor it, they would no longer be tempted to contend for false privileges; and fraternity could then be born between them (p. 12).

Flesh and spirit, neither inferior nor superior to one another, the partners in romantic love are united by a bond of mutuality, not by attempts to set oneself up as a demigod to be worshipped by the other as a source of right or wrong; good or bad; true or false. In the latter environment of "false privilege," it is impossible to attain the soulful resonance and harmony that is requisite to romantic love.

On the other hand, seeing each other as peers, each with subjective lives, as well as corporeal ones, the foundation for (mutual) empathetic understanding is set. My subjectivity—the overall gestalt of feelings, wishes, desires, or thoughts that comprise my "mind"—is no truer, better, or more important than yours *simply because it is my subjectivity*. And yours is no more important than mine *simply because it is yours*. Accordingly, mutual sharing of our subjective worlds can proceed on an equal (epistemic) footing. Exploring your felt meanings is no less respectable or morally incumbent than exploring mine, and conversely.

During a particularly rough day, I sense your desire for a safe respite in my arms and I extend my arms and embrace you for a moment, tenderly stroke your long dark hair as I know you like, and then kiss you gently on your delicate lips. You gaze into my eyes, and I feel your presence deep inside my soul. You smile warmly, knowingly; lightly kiss my lips; then gracefully recede like the fading conclusion of a love song. Herein are the sensual point and counterpoint of a well-orchestrated duet, one that could never be performed by a soloist playing exclusively to their own subjectivity.

Living only in one's own subjective world is solitary and lonely

There are, perhaps, no better philosophical reflections to illustrate the desolate feelings of such a solipsistic existence than that of the French seventeenth-century philosopher, Rene Descartes. Many of us have heard of Descartes' idea that "I think therefore I am." With this now-famous pronouncement, Descartes (2001) sought to prove his very own existence beyond the shadow of a doubt. For, how could one even doubt one's existence and not exist! Accordingly, Descartes concluded, "it must, in fine, be maintained […] that this proposition *I am, I exist*, is necessarily true each time it is expressed by me or conceived in my mind" (Meditation 2).

It is something like this bit of curious logic that leads us to feel assured of our own existence every time we catch ourselves in the act of thinking. So, our own subjective existence (our thoughts plus the ego, or self, having these thoughts) seems to be the starting point from which to construct our worldviews.

Unfortunately, the ego-obsessive individual does not faithfully venture outside their own subjective existence to recognize other subjective existences as veridical, besides their own. This is what philosophers call the "solipsistic position," and it is what Descartes himself sought to escape through his meditative philosophy. How do I know, asked Descartes, whether what I take to be other minds and the physical world outside me do not merely exist *inside me* as "modes of consciousness" (Meditation 3)?

I will not recount, here, the philosophical twists and turns Descartes exercised to break out of his solipsism to prove the existence of external minds and bodies. In the end, Descartes' dogged determination to escape this profoundly lonely and solitary existence underscores the importance of venturing outside one's own subjectivity to find peace of mind and personal happiness.

Acknowledge the legitimacy of other people's subjectivity, not just your own, or lose your sanity

Most philosophers do not believe that Descartes managed to prove with certitude that such an external world outside one's own subjectivity even exists.

Instead, such belief may, more realistically, be based on what Spanish American philosopher, George Santayana (1923), called "animal faith." Thus spoke this philosopher in stark terms:

> Perception points to what it does not [...] know to exist; knowledge is only of the past or the future, both of which are absent; and intelligence talks and talks to an interlocutor—the mind of another man or god or an eventual self of one's own—whom it can never see and whose replies, conveyed (if at all) through material channels, it is never sure exist morally, or could be understood if they did exist. There is no dilemma in the choice between animal faith and reason, because reason is only a form of animal faith, and utterly unintelligible dialectically, although full of a pleasant alacrity and confidence, like the chirping of birds. The suasion of sanity is physical: if you cut your animal traces, you run mad (p. 260).

Santayana would even question Descartes' "I think therefore I exist," maintaining that belief in one's own subjective existence is also an unprovable matter of animal faith (p. 41). Such faith is not itself founded on reason because reason is itself a form of animal faith for Santayana. To the ego-obsessive individual who refuses to validate the subjective existences of others, Santayana's message is clear and blunt: Accept on animal faith the legitimacy of other subjective existences or "run mad"!

So, you don't really need proof that the subjective existence of others—their thoughts, feelings, desires, fears, wishes, hopes, dreams, and the rest of psychic life—carries epistemic status. Run amok too often and you lose your sanity. Denounce your partner's legitimate claims to have their subjectivity dignified and you can expect a relationship fraught with contentious and unmitigated contempt, resentment, frustration, or other forms of inward or outward hostility. Your salvation lies in giving up the self-destructive demand to invent and impose your subjective reality on others who may see things otherwise.

In proclaiming reality by fiat, you also deprive yourself of the opportunity to gain the insights of others and to engage in meaningful and productive dialog with them. Your ideas may be bankrupt and lead to great unhappiness for both you and your partner even if unconditionally imposed and accepted. Instead, successful relationships are often the product of cooperative effort and teamsmanship. Any attempt at cultivating romantic love is squandered on someone who resists such efforts in favor of solipsistic exclusion of all but their own subjectivity.

The individual, separate self is an illusion

To break out of your solipsistic exclusion where yours is the only subjectivity you accept, you will need to accept others as you accept yourself. In true love, this means the person you love. According to Buddhist monk, Thich Nhat Hanh (2015),

> In true love, there's no more separation or discrimination. His happiness is your happiness. Your suffering is his suffering. You can no longer say, "That's your problem." In true love, both happiness and suffering are no longer individual matters. You are him, and he is you (p. 50).

Of course, we are human beings, and, like the rest of us, true lovers do sometimes get caught up in spats and experience disunifying emotions such as jealousy, anger, and impatience. However, the tendency among true lovers is to experience intersubjective unity. Thus, the suffering of your partner is just as real as your suffering. Indeed, as lovers, your suffering is my suffering. This means that, as your true love, I must transcend preoccupation with my own subjectivity, and resonate with your subjective reality as my own. Seeing with one set of eyes, your self and mine, comprises a broader collective self.

This is the Buddhist doctrine sometimes referred to as the doctrine of "non-self." According to Hanh (2015),

> Often, when we say, "I love you" we focus mostly on the idea of the "I" who is doing the loving and less on the quality of the love that's being offered […]. But there is no such thing as an individual separate self. A flower is made only of non-flower elements, such as chlorophyll, sunlight, and water […]. Humans are like this too. We can't exist by ourselves alone. We can only inter-be. I am made only of non-me elements, such as the Earth, the sun, parents, and ancestors (p. 92).

So, in true love, you and your partner are interbeings whose suffering is one. For the Buddhist, this broader sense of self, composed of our interbeing, is the true sense. The self as it exists apart from all else (the one commonly denoted by the words, "I," "me," and "mine") is simply an illusion likely resulting from our brains leading us to think in terms of our own subjectivity rather than our broader inclusive subjective interbeing. The latter inclusive sense of subjective being makes possible a selfless sense of compassion for your partner.

The compassion you feel, based on attachment (to "I," "me," or "mine"), is different than that which you feel when you truly love someone

This sense of selfless compassion is distinct from compassion that is focused on oneself rather than the other. Thus, I could feel compassion for my partner's suffering because they are *my* partner. Such attachment to the object of compassion (that is, my partner) is not a transcendent, selfless type of compassion. This is because it is contingent on whether my partner remains my partner, and whether they continue to satisfy certain of my self-interested desires, expectations, or purposes. Hence, this type of compassion cannot support enduring, romantic love, which, hyperbolically stated, is eternal and immutable, transcending time and place, indelibly written in the heavens.

The venerable Dalai Lama (2009) succinctly draws the distinction:

> First, I think that there is a different quality between the feeling of genuine love, or compassion, and love based on attachment. It's not the same feeling. The feeling of genuine compassion is much stronger, much wider; it has a very profound quality. Also, genuine love and compassion are much more stable, more reliable (p. 116).

According to the Dalai Lama, this genuine type of compassion for the suffering of another is attained only if one appreciates the seriousness and intensity of the other's suffering. This does not mean that one is overwhelmed or feels helpless in experiencing the suffering of another, as you might be in the case of experiencing your own suffering. "Rather, although you feel discomfort in the other's suffering, there is a feeling of connectedness and commitment, a willingness to reach out to others, a feeling of freshness rather than dullness" (pp. 117–118). The Dalai Lama compares this to an athlete who experiences pain in working out but sees a higher purpose in the training, which in turn alters the quality of the experience.

In being self-obsessive, you deprive yourself of the opportunity to acquiesce in this form of compassion. You may find yourself feeling upset by your partner's suffering, wanting your partner to feel better. But this is largely because you want your own discomfort to stop so you don't have to be put out emotionally or behaviorally by it. Thus, you may desire your partner's happiness because it is not comfortable to be in a relationship with an unhappy partner. The intrinsic quality of caring, the connectedness you feel with your partner's well-being, and the commitment you have, to helping your partner feel better for its own sake, is simply not there. So how can you achieve this state of selfless resonance with your partner?

Focus your attention on friendship, compassion, delight, and equanimity toward others

According to the *Yoga Sutras* of the ancient Indian sage, Patanjali, the key to such a state of true love is detachment from the "I," "me," and "mine." "Consciousness settles," says Patanjali (2003), "as one radiates friendliness, compassion, delight, and equanimity toward all things, whether pleasant or painful, good or bad" (p. 99). The main idea here is to take focus off oneself onto the other; such that, in "focusing with perfect discipline on friendliness, compassion, delight, and equanimity, one is imbued with their energies" (p. 106). Demonstrating each of these four virtues—friendliness, compassion, delight, and equanimity—in the appropriate context can help build genuine love in your relationship. If your partner is having a bad day, then you can radiate "compassion" for them. If they are happy, due to good fortune, then you can exude "friendliness" by rejoicing in their happiness. If they are exhibiting virtue, for example, doing a kind act, then you can radiate "delight" (appreciation) for what they have done. If they do something improper, for example, something you believe to be unfair, then you can show "equanimity" by not judging *the person* of your partner even though you may disagree with their action. In each case, your attitude is one of intrinsic regard, that is, you demonstrate unconditional acceptance of your partner, whether they are happy, sad, or behave virtuously or unvirtuously. In this way, these four virtues cover the gamut of circumstances that partners invariably confront in their relationship.

Recalling how they are suffering now or in the past, you can open your heart to what they are going through (or have gone through) in their own subjective consciousness—their fears, insecurities, struggles, and disappointments. Never minding whether you agree or disagree with their feelings, absorbing your own consciousness into theirs, pushing gently aside any distracting thoughts. In this meditative state, you send a message of loving kindness to your partner such as "May you be safe," "May you be peaceful"; "May you be healthy"; or "May you live with ease and wellbeing," depending on which message best resonates with your subjective awareness of your partner's suffering. Repeating your loving kindness mantra, while resonating with your partner's experience, you feel the connectedness you have with them arising from the compassion that is emanating from you (Bloomfield, 2020).

Building compassion for your partner is not possible in a social vacuum, however. Indeed, your capacity for genuinely expressing loving kindness for your partner is strengthened when you also radiate loving kindness for others. This means expanding the range of those you express loving kindness to. Thus, you could start by sending your loving kindness message to others you are close to, such as your friends and family. Then send it to others you are not close to but have not disliked. Next, send it to others you have disliked or not gotten along with. Finally, having worked up to it, you could then send your message of loving kindness to *all* humankind, close or distant, known or unknown, friend or foe. It is serene, indeed, to feel the partitions that separate you from all others evaporating. So that when you meet your partner, in the bedroom, or the commerce of your everyday life together, the love you bring to the relationship is not diluted or distracted by unkind feelings for others. Instead, it is fortified by a loving kindness that has no limits or barriers.

Suspend doubt temporarily to understand the other's perspective instead of coming at it with doubt and incredulity

This Yoga-based process of connecting is, in turn, supported by a feminist epistemology developed by Mary Field Belenky et al. (1997) in their seminal work, *Women's Ways of Knowing*. In this work, these authors distinguish between "connected knowing" and "separate knowing" (p. 100). The latter involves trying to find the truth by looking at others' perspectives with doubt and incredulity, trying to find fallacies or other flaws on the basis of which to reject them. For example: "Aren't you contradicting yourself by saying you want a good relationship while complaining so much?"

Indeed, it was by applying this "separate" way of knowing that Descartes painted himself into a solipsistic corner—that is, by trying to doubt everything that he could possibly find reason to doubt, including subjective existences other than his own. Along similar lines, you might ask your partner, "Why should I put any credence in what you are saying when I can't even be certain that you're not trying to deceive me?" So, like Descartes, you may find yourself, gazing into a dark epistemic void, feeling forlorn, trusting only in your own subjective reality to the exclusion of that of others.

In contrast, "connected knowing" involves searching for the truth by suspending doubt temporarily to understand the other's perspective. "I can understand how you would be really pissed at me if you thought I was unfaithful." Here, instead of trying to convince my partner that there is no rational basis for them to be angry in the first place, I do my level best to first understand why they are so angry at me. In this way, I connect with them, recognizing the legitimacy of their feelings, instead of becoming self-defensive and destroying the prospect of sharing our subjective realities.

There is, then, the opportunity to bring out certain facts that can help promote a resolution to the conflict. "Oh, I see, you thought that I was with my ex that night I came home late. I had no idea they were telling others that we were back together again. I would have felt the same way, but it's just not true. I was very clear to them that it was over between us, and that I was in love with you." Thus, instead of straightaway dismissing my partner's subjective existence as groundless, I attempt to understand, indeed embrace it. As a result, we connect, and I learn new information that helps to create new shared meanings and mutual acceptance of our respective, subjective existences.

Identifying Some Core Philosophical Aspects of Empathy

As discussed in the last chapter, not every philosophical approach to overcoming impediments to romantic love will work for everyone, so you don't need to buy wholesale any philosophy. Nevertheless, there are aspects of the philosophies discussed in this chapter that are essential to overcoming the tendency to be ego-obsessive, cultivate empathy, and thus find intimacy in romantic love. Here are some important ones:

- The starting point of your partner's reality is their subjective existence, just like the starting point of your reality is your subjective reality.
- Your subjectivity—the overall gestalt of feelings, wishes, desires, or thoughts that comprise your "mind"—is no truer, better, or more important than your partner's simply because it is your subjectivity, and your partner's is no more important than yours simply because it is your partner's.
- You are both human, which means that you are both flesh and blood, mortal, and subject to the same physical forces in nature.
- Being trapped in a solipsistic universe, trapped inside your own subjectivity, where your subjective existence is the only one that counts, is a lonely existence, indeed,

- Believing in your partner's subjective existence as true, or worthy of respect, is an article of faith, nothing you can prove. Deny it too often, however, and you risk losing your sanity, let alone never finding true love.
- Meaningful and productive dialog with your partner assumes such respect.
- Obsession with "I," "me," and "mine" destroys the prospect of the unity of souls (or the coalescence of separate subjective beings) that is essential to finding romantic love.
- If you make your love dependent on whether it satisfies your own self-interest, you will fail to find the transcendent eternality or foreverness quality of romantic love, reaching no further than a relationship of convenience with sexual benefits.
- In attempting to experience your partner's suffering, you don't need to be overwhelmed by it; for it has a higher purpose of connectedness, which pervades the experience.
- Demonstrate unconditional acceptance of your partner through friendliness, compassion, delight, and equanimity. Participating in their happiness when things go well for them. Key into and be there for them in their time of suffering. Be appreciative when they act virtuously; and be nonjudgmental of them as a person when they behave badly, even though you may, in no uncertain terms, disapprove of the deed.
- You are not likely to tend toward the latter four virtues if you do not also extend them to others besides your partner.
- Being open to the subjective reality of your partner (or that of others) means suspending doubt as a way of seeking truth. This does not mean that, in the end, you should believe what you know to be false. Rather, you can suspend doubt, temporarily, to connect with your partner, seeing things from their perspective, then using this understanding to come to more enlightened conclusions about the truth.

Applying the Eclectic Philosophy Through Cognitive-Behavioral Practice

Applying these philosophical frames requires practice. This means using them to reframe your ego-centric perspectives in relating to your partner. You can work toward this goal by doing the cognitive-behavioral exercises and applying the guidelines I have provided for building empathy in your everyday life:

EXERCISE 1

Practicing Empathy

Empathy is a virtue, which means it is a habit, which means you can get better at it through practice! Give yourself some practice by doing the following:

- Find a time to meet with your partner about an issue they are having—something that pertains to their perceived welfare, interest, or need. For example, maybe they are upset about a matter at work. It could be something relating to your relationship, but this is probably something to work up to since it's a lot harder to maintain distance when the issue directly concerns you.
- Key into human values you share. For example, you both know what it's like to be treated unfairly.
- Suspend, temporarily, your own considered judgments and critiques. So, even if you disagree with your partner about something, you will need to psychologically bracket this by putting it out of your mind. Don't try to fix things, either, because empathizing is not about fixing things. It's about letting your partner share their subjective world with you and having their right to it validated by you.
- To validate this right, you will need to connect with your partner's subjective world. This means putting yourself in their subjective world, saying "Yes" to it, and busting your gut to see the truth in it. Again, this is not about looking for flaws in what they are saying or feeling.
- Use reflection to help clarify what your partner is saying. For example, if your partner tells you that their boss is constantly finding fault with their work, you might say "So you feel like your boss is not appreciating the good work you are doing."
- Listen carefully to what your partner is telling you, without lecturing or talking at your partner. This is about giving your partner an opportunity to express their feelings and ideas, not a time to tell them the way it is.

(*Continued*)

- Use self-disclosure only if it is relevant to what your partner is saying and it is not excessive. Be careful not to take the focus off your partner and onto yourself.
- Properly distance yourself to and from your partner's subjective world.

For more discussion regarding the above guidelines, please read the following article, I have written for *Psychology Today* (Cohen, 2015):
https://www.psychologytoday.com/us/blog/what-would-aristotle-do/201505/how-be-empathetic
Keep practicing!

EXERCISE 2

Loving Kindness Meditation

Loving Kindness meditation, as discussed in this chapter, is an excellent way to build compassion for your partner. To get you started, I suggest following the 20-minute guided "Loving Kindness Meditation" audio by Dr Kristin Neff (n.d.) accessible online at https://self-compassion.org/guided-self-compassion-meditations-mp3-2

Keep in mind that loving your partner also means loving yourself as well as others, so you will also want to include yourself as well as others when sending out your loving kindness message.

Guidelines for Building Empathy

- Strongly push yourself to connect with your partner by understanding your partner's subjective reality rather than trying to find things wrong with it, or with your partner. You will not succeed in empathizing with them to the extent that you do the latter.
- Strongly push yourself to let your partner own their own values without attempting to force your own values on them.
- Practice loving-kindness meditation regularly by sending messages of loving kindness to yourself, your partner, and others. (See the second featured activity.)
- Practice mindfulness meditation. This is a good way to help you detach from your focus on "I," "me," or "mine" by instead nonjudgmentally focusing on

something else, such as your breathing, or other object. I suggest following the Palouse course featured in Chapter 1.
- Practice reflective listening, as described earlier in this chapter, reflecting back in insightful ways what your partner has disclosed to you.
- Practice the four virtues of friendliness, compassion, delight, and equanimity in appropriate contexts as described earlier in this chapter. For example, when your partner acts in a way you take to be insensitive, unfair, or unkind, refrain from your usual routine of personally attacking them. Instead, convey to them your disapproval of what they have said or done, not of them as a person.
- Accept responsibility when you make mistakes or act inappropriately instead of attempting to pass yourself off as being beyond human fallibility. Keep in mind, de Beauvoir's admonition that both you and your partner are human, and hence not beyond human fallibility.
- Practice sharing your partner's meanings when they are experiencing misfortune (so-called "negative empathy"). This means practicing the other skills included in this section such as:
  - Reflective listening;
  - Expressing loving-kindness;
  - Mindfully pushing distracting thoughts about yourself away to focus on their subjective world;
  - Refraining from denying the reality or legitimacy of their feelings, values, hopes, expectations, desires, etc.;
  - Instead, conveying to them the right to own their subjective reality; and
  - Strongly pushing yourself to understand rather than criticize this reality.
- Resonate with your partner through shared experiences. Perhaps you have had a similar experience as your partner, and you can understand what they are going through because of having had this experience. Self-disclosure to connect can be helpful in such a case if it is relevant to your partner's situation, and you are not using the disclosure to work through your own issues. Otherwise, the focus is not on your partner's subjective reality but instead on your own, which forecloses the possibility of empathic understanding of your partner's plight.

Practicing in these ways, you can start to build intimacy with your partner; overcoming the tendency to preoccupy yourself with your own subjective existence to the exclusion of that of your partner; resonating with your partner's felt meanings, building the empathic relationship that is essential for enduring, romantic love.

When lovers are in such resonance, there is a climate of unity, two as one, that is the condition of romantic love. This unity is consummated in the bedroom where, as Plato would say, two souls, "are melded into one soul," with their bodies coming together harmonically pulsating as one. To use a Neoplatonic metaphor, the practice of empathy is the way the soul is "purified" in preparation for the mystical ascent into the heaven of enduring, romantic love. It is preliminary to the attainment of the soulful ecstasy attained through making love, not merely the sensual, mechanical bliss of having sex.

Such ecstasy is not attained among those who are self-denigrating. Thus, a lover who harbors low self-esteem is unlikely to find enduring, romantic love in the arms of another—unless they overcome their low self-esteem. Accordingly, the next chapter addresses the latter impediment, along with its guiding virtue and set of profoundly important philosophical ideas you can apply both inside and outside the bedroom.

References

Aristotle. 2000. *Metaphysics*, Trans. W. D. Ross. Internet Classics Archive. https://classics.mit.edu/Aristotle/metaphysics.mb.txt.

Belenky, Mary Field, Clinchy, Blythe Mcvicker, Goldberger, Nancy Rule, Mattuck, Jill. 1997. *Women's Ways of Knowing: The Development of Self, Voice, and Mind*. New York: Basic Books.

Bloomfield, Marie. 2020. "Loving kindness meditation for couples." Mindfulpath. https://www.mindfulpath.com.au/application/files/3115/8231/7644/Loving_kindness_for_couple.pdf.

Cohen, Elliot D. 2015, May 17. "How to be empathetic: Find out what you can do to improve your relationships." *Psychology Today*. https://www.psychologytoday.com/us/blog/what-would-aristotle-do/201505/how-be-empathetic.

Dalai Lama & Cutler, Howard C. 2009. *The Art of Happiness*. New York: Penguin Publishing Group (Kindle ed). https://www.amazon.com/Art-Happiness-10th-Anniversary-Handbook-ebook/dp/B002UK6NO0.

De Beauvoir, Simone. 2010. *The Second Sex*. New York: Random House.

Descartes, Rene. 2001. *Meditations on First Philosophy*, Trans. J. Veitch. Classical Library. http://www.classicallibrary.org/descartes/meditations/.

Hanh, Tich Nhat. 2015. *How to Love*. Berkeley, CA: Parallax Press.

Mount Sinai Medical Center. 2012, October 24. "Area of the Brain that Processes Empathy Identified." *Science Daily*. https://www.sciencedaily.com/releases/2012/10/121024175240.htm.

Patanjali. 2003. *The Yoga-Sutra of Patanjali*. Shambhala Classics (Kindle ed.). https://www.amazon.com/Yoga-Sutras-Patanjali-ebook/dp/B00JXLGG2I.

Neff, Kristin. n.d. "Loving-Kindness Meditation: Self-Compassion." Self-Compassion.org. https://self-compassion.org/guided-self-compassion-%20meditations-mp3-2/.

Rogers, Carl R. 1974. Carl Rogers on Empathy (Whitely, J.M., Producer), Distinguished Contributors to Counseling Film Series. American Personnel and Guidance Association [American Counseling Association]. https://video.alexanderstreet.com/watch/carl-rogerson-empathy-part-1.

Santayana, George. 1923. *Skepticism and Animal Faith: Introduction to a System of Philosophy.* New York: Charles Scribner.

CHAPTER 3

BUILDING SELF-RESPECT AND RESPECT FOR OTHERS IN ROMANTIC LOVE

[I]n marriage there is generally a component of emotional attachment. But I think that if there is a component of genuine compassion as well, based on mutual respect as two human beings, the marriage tends to last a long time.

—Dalai Lama, *The Art of Happiness*

Recognizing Self- and Other-Damning Thoughts as Impediments

Damning yourself

If you tell yourself that you are unworthy, then you have, by that very pronouncement, fulfilled your own prophecy; for in telling yourself this, you have set yourself up to fail. "I can't find true love in the arms of another because no one could ever love someone like me." You have effectively decided your own fate. Some people who self-damn intentionally act in ways that would turn the other off. After all, isn't a failure supposed to act like one!? So, you may play the role of a failure, doing exactly what *won't* build an enduring, loving relationship. Such self-sabotage becomes a way of life, such that many who play this self-defeating game waste much, if not all their lives undermining their relationships with others.

In his classic book, *Games People Play*, psychologist Erich Berne (1964) speaks of a "life script" in which people create situations leading to negative feelings that they can, in turn, use to advance their life scripts (p. 2). The self-sabotaging person sets things up so that they can continue to reaffirm in their mind that they are a failure. This is a vicious game to play since the more the person plays it, the more they give themselves a reason to keep playing it!

Others may suffer from the so-called, "imposture syndrome" wherein they secretly tell themselves they are unworthy of others' respect or approval and, as a result, feel like frauds when others think highly of them (Cohen, 2022). Such individuals tend to be perfectionists who damn themselves when they fall short of achieving perfection—as they inevitably do.

In some cases, these individuals may display narcissistic tendencies by being braggadocious, vain, pretentious, or pompous, while feeling insecure about their own self-worth. These behaviors may be an attempt to get rid of their feelings of insecurity by attempting to convince themselves—as well as others—that they are extraordinarily worthy people.

Other self-damning individuals may demand the approval of others and tend to damn themselves when they do not gain this approval. Such individuals constantly experience anxiety because the approval of others (even if they presently have it) depends on the whims of others as well as on the individual's perceived ability to maintain this approval. The approval in question may be that of a certain set of "special" people such as one's partner or one's boss. In some cases, however, the approval of others *in general* may be sought, so that even being "given the middle finger" by an irate motorist may cast aspersions on the individual's sense of self-worth.

In still other cases, the self-damning person may attempt to put others down to elevate themselves. Thus, such individuals play the game of looking for a "blemish" in others to soothe themselves (Berne, p. 48). For example, the white Aryan racist who discriminates against Blacks and Jews may attempt to deal with their own low self-esteem by engaging in various degrees of discrimination. Such discrimination may range from speaking pejoratively about these groups in closed social gatherings to publicly denouncing them, joining racist gangs and organizations, and perpetrating violent acts against them (Allport, 1979).

In all the above cases, the self-damning person is not likely to find enduring true love because they will self-sabotage or alienate their partner. If I try to cleanse myself of my low self-esteem by putting my partner down, the obvious result will be a dysfunctional relationship characterized by anxiety and resentment. In bed, I will be the critic, not the lover. "It's you, not me, who needs to be more creative."

If you suffer from imposture syndrome, then you will see any failure, in the bedroom or outside it, as evidence that you are truly not worthy of your partner's love. Feeling guilty, and seeing yourself as a fraud, you may attempt to get rid of your guilty feelings. For example, you may do something to let your partner know just how inferior you really are such as acting mean-spirited or maybe even having an affair!

If you demand your partner's approval to feel good about yourself, then you may constantly be on the lookout for signs that your partner is withdrawing his approval. For example, as soon as your partner becomes preoccupied with something else, you may take it as a sign that they no longer love you. There is thus the perceived "need" for constant attention such that any attention directed away from you is taken as abandonment, as a sign that you have lost your partner's approval.

If you attempt to prove to your partner how wonderful you are, so that you can feel better about yourself, then your self-absorbedness will predictably leave your partner feeling alone without someone who truly understands their desires or wants. You may thereby drive a wedge between the two of you, making impossible, or unlikely, the comingling and unity, sexually and spiritually, that is emblematic of romantic love.

In any event, you are likely to place a serious strain on your relationship and potential for cultivating enduring, romantic love, unless you overcome the tendency to damn yourself.

Damning others

Many people who have low self-esteem also damn others. Somehow, they think they can rid themselves of their inferiority by projecting it onto others. This defense mechanism only creates further dysfunction in interpersonal relationships. The partner who constantly puts down his partner to make themselves look taller, especially in social contexts, merely succeeds in making themselves look smaller. This process of projecting one's own disavowed attributes onto another, known as "projective identification," is often unconscious (Yalom & Leszcz, 2020, 443). So, you may yourself have doubts about your own intelligence and project this onto your partner by calling them "stupid."

Damning others is often a way to degrade them so that they can be mistreated. It is not unusual to find a person calling another person a dirty word only to then do something destructive to them. Clearly, language that has a negative valence can come in handy for those who would like to act aggressively toward others. As psychologist Albert Bandura keenly stated,

> Self-sanctions against cruel conduct can be disengaged or blunted by divesting people of human qualities. Once dehumanized, they are no longer viewed as persons with feelings, hopes, and concerns but as subhuman objects. They are portrayed as mindless 'savages', 'gooks', 'satanic fiends', and the like. Subhumans are regarded as insensitive to maltreatment and capable

of being influenced only by harsh methods. If dispossessing antagonists of humanness does not blunt self-reproof, it can be eliminated by attributing bestial qualities to them. It is easier to brutalize victims, for example, when they are referred to as 'worms' (Bandura, 1990, 180).

In dysfunctional relationships where there are power differentials, pejorative epithets such as "no good," "son-of-a-bitch," "piece of crap," and even worse—is used to justify the mistreatment of the other party. If someone is truly "trash," then it is not wrong to dispose of the person in some way or other. So, instead of a guilty conscience, for having mistreated another person, the aggressive party has a dirty name to somehow vindicate the mistreatment. "She's a lowly whore and got just what she deserved."

It is often stated that sticks and stones can break your bones, but names can never harm you. This is not the case. In many dysfunctional, abusive relationships, a dominant member of a couple may use pejorative labels to victimize the more vulnerable member. Tell a person long enough that they are stupid and unworthy, and they will begin to believe this of themselves or start to entertain self-doubts. Sadly, I have seen many women (and some men as well) have their sense of self-esteem eviscerated, or further eroded, by having teamed up with such a perpetrator.

In fact, much of what is called "victim mentality" (Gepp & Lebow, 2022) is a function of negative self-assessment arising from such negative attribution by others. As a child, did a parent convey the message to you that you were unworthy? Pejorative labels are not the only way in which such conveyance is possible. For example, the parent may have been hypercritical of you, finding fault with most things you did, implying, if not stating, that "You can't do anything right!" Here, the message is clear. You are unworthy, even if negative epithets are not used. Then, the child does something degrading, as would be expected of someone who believed they were incapable of anything else. Maybe they get into trouble at school (get into fights) or with the law (take illegal drugs or steal a car), and thus receive corroboration of their unworthiness, thereby reinforcing their negative self-image. This is not to mention other ways in which a parent can degrade a child, such as physical and sexual abuse.

Not uncommonly, people who are involved in abusive relationships as adults, either as perpetrators or as victims, are survivors of abusive treatment as children (Lünnemann et al., 2019). These couples then, in turn, have children who grow up in abusive households and themselves subsequently become perpetrators or victims. Thus, abusive relationships are intergenerational. Abuse spawns further abuse.

Abusive households are clearly not conducive to the cultivation of enduring, romantic love (Gills, 2022). On the contrary, such relationships tend to breed a lack of candor, distrust, disrespect, loss of self-control, and cowardice. If you were brought up in such an abusive environment, then you may be bringing with you, to your present relationship, tendencies acquired because of having lived through such trauma. Most remarkably, these would include tendencies to put yourself or others down (Pereira et al., 2021). Becoming aware of such a tendency and resolving to do something about it is the first step toward constructive change.

Identifying Respect for Self and Others as Counters to Self- and Other-Damnation

It is said that to love others one must also love oneself. As social psychologist Erich Fromm (2006) states,

> [M]y own self must be as much an object of my love as another person. *The affirmation of one's own life, happiness, growth, freedom is rooted in one's capacity to love* i.e. in care, respect, responsibility, and knowledge. If an individual is able to love productively, he loves himself too; if he can love *only* others, he cannot love at all. (pp. 55–56, emphasis is original)

To love oneself in this way, however, is the opposite of narcissism. Narcissists are incapable of loving others and hence are incapable of loving themselves. They view love as something to possess and control. They declare the terms of love and decide whether others are worthy of their love. They are dictators and dictators take no partners. But love is a partnership, not totalitarianism, so narcissists cannot love others. Nor, therefore, can they love themselves, for self-love, no less than the love of others, is not a matter of fiat. The narcissist, however, dictates his own superiority. They declare themselves the supreme being, incapable of fault, the best of the best, the infallible, the wisest, and most accomplished. But such self-exaltation is delusional, not reality. Their "self-love" is thus deceptive, counterfeit, and bogus. Perhaps it is low self-esteem camouflaged by over-grandiosity, or perhaps it is simply pathological egotism, but it is clearly not truly self-love; and the latter is requisite to loving others.

This is no less true in romantic love than in any other form of love. To be in love with another is not to be infatuated or obsessed with another because you think they can somehow remediate some defect or otherwise supply something missing from you. It is not to perceive your own self-worth as a function of the one you think you love. To be truly in love is to meet the other as a person in their own right. This means that you perceive them as a locus of intrinsic worth and dignity that supports, as well as is supported by, the other person in a seamless integration of intrinsic value. Here the whole is greater than the sum of the parts.

However, the two in love are also independent, not codependent. They do not come together because they perceive themselves as unworthy or dysfunctional without each other. They do not come together so that one can assert dominion over the other. On the contrary, they come together because they consider themselves equally worthy of uniting as one. Thus, away from each other, in the commerce of daily life, such as at their respective workplaces, they enjoy an independent, functional existence as well.

In the bedroom, I am not a leach that sucks you dry and jumps off when there is nothing left to suck. I do not feed off you like a parasite. Instead, in the act of making love, the "we" of "me" and "you" temporarily coalesces into oneness. To be sure, there is pleasure, but it is not *my* pleasure or *yours*; it is not even *our* pleasure; but rather ecstatic unity. Mystics such as Plotinus (1956) capture this idea well in speaking about the mystical ecstasy arising in experiencing God. It is in this experience where the partitions that separate you from the divine evaporate leaving behind the ineffable, ecstatic experience of unity with the divine.

There is indeed a mystical ecstatic experience involved in the act of making love. This cannot happen if you or I are leeches or parasites. Like the ecstatic experience of the divine spoken by Plotinus, you and I must be prepared for it. According to Plotinus, to experience the divine, one must have attained virtue—such as prudence and courage. Similarly, you and I must both be self-respecting, functional, independent beings. Without such virtue, mutually possessed, neither you nor I are in any condition to make love in the bedroom or to forge an enduring, romantic love.

This set of virtues is that of respect for yourself and others. Psychologist Albert Ellis defines such respect in terms of *unconditional self and other acceptance* (Ellis, 2001, p. 84). This means that you do not base your self-worth or the worth of others on how well you or they perform but rather accept yourself and others regardless of how well you or they perform. This does not mean that you must accept what you or others do or say. Indeed, there is a difference between accepting the person and accepting what the person says or does. Thus, I can totally reject something you said as false or misguided without rejecting you. Similarly, I can love you without loving everything you do. But I do not make my love of you, or myself, conditional on whether I approve of what you, or I, do.

Carl R. Rogers (1995) compares such love to the love of a parent for a child. Thus, the parent does not stop loving the child when the child does something wrong (say, writing all over the walls with indelible markers). The parent can be justified in condemning the deed. "What you did was unacceptable." This is not the same as telling the child that *they* are unacceptable. On the contrary, to unconditionally accept the child means that the child continues to be accepted by the parent even though the parent does not accept what the child has done.

There is also a reciprocal relation between unconditional acceptance of others and oneself. As Ellis (2001) astutely observed, when people fully accept themselves, they also tend to fully accept all other people, and vice versa. They also excel in achieving their personal goals and in their interpersonal relationships. As previously mentioned, people who damn themselves often damn others (by looking for their "blemishes") to make themselves feel better. On the other hand, in unconditionally accepting yourself, you come to rightly see that the worth of all human beings is independent of any perceived defects. As such, in embracing self-respect, you can also come to respect others, unconditionally, and thus overcome a chief obstacle to building enduring, romantic love.

Embracing respect for self and others, *unconditionally*, means that you tend to think of yourself and others as worthy of respect, regardless of how well you/ they perform. It does not depend on others' approval, or on the amount of money one has. Sexual orientation or race does not matter. It does not depend on whether one fits a media-generated concept of physical attractiveness, or any number of other things that people have used to demoralize, torment, and degrade themselves or others.

Unfortunately, many people have spent most of their lives thinking about their own worth and that of others precisely in such self-defeating terms. Consequently, they have undermined their prospect of attaining enduring, romantic love, not to mention personal and interpersonal happiness in other respects. Needed, then, is the *philosophical* reframing of your own and your partner's worth conducive to attaining respect for self and others understood as unconditional acceptance of self and others.

Philosophies that Build Respect for Self and Others

Treat others, and yourself, as ends in themselves (persons), not as mere means (objects)

According to philosopher Immanuel Kant (2004), as human beings, we are all *persons*. To be a person, he says, is to be a rational being, that is, an *autonomous* being with the capacity to make one's own decisions based on one's capacity to reason. For Kant, this ability to engage in rational self-determination makes human beings quite special, indeed. For example, physical objects do not possess such an extraordinary ability. Rather, they are *heteronomous*, that is, determined by things outside themselves. For example, I have used my computer to produce the textual context of this book. What my computer writes is what I direct it to write. And if the computer ceases to perform the functions for which I use it, I am free to discard it and purchase a new one. Indeed, unless my computer does what it is designed to do, it ceases to have any value for me, and I am justified in discarding it or trading it in for a new computer.

According to Kant, this is not how we should look at human beings, whether ourselves or others. Thus, I should not discard another human being when they cease to serve some purpose that I have for them. This is because human beings, unlike mere physical objects, are *persons*; therefore, they have rights, especially the right to self-determination. This means that I must first ask people for their consent before manipulating or using them, in any way. As the owner of my computer, I can do what I wish with it. The idea of getting the computer's consent is not sensible—not unless or until computers become rational, self-determining beings!

In the bedroom, your partner is not a computer that is programmed to respond in certain ways. Nor do you own your partner. For they are a *person*, a rational, self-determining being, capable of expressing and exercising their own wishes and desires. Nonconsensual manipulation of your partner's body is thus not part of making love. This is to confuse a person with an object. It is a violation of your partner's personhood or right of self-determination. Indeed, this is precisely what makes rape such a heinous crime. It robs the victim of their right to self-determination, which is what makes us *persons*.

Human beings thus have *intrinsic* worth and dignity, in contrast to objects such as computers. The latter have *instrumental* worth, meaning that they are useful for attaining certain purposes. When they cease to fulfill their purposes, they cease to have value. Unlike objects, the value that human beings have is *unconditional*. It does not depend on whether the individual is useful for this or that purpose.

Is your relationship with your partner based exclusively on your partner's performing certain sexual acts that you enjoy, such as oral stimulation or sadomasochistic acts? Consequently, would you abandon the relationship if they were unable or refused to perform these acts? If so, you are not capable of making love to her. You may be having satisfying, even highly orgasmic sex, but you are not making love. This is because you do not value your partner as a person, but instead as a thing that can sexually stimulate you.

"But isn't that what having sex is all about?" Yes, *just* having sex, but it is not what *making love* is all about. The latter requires a conceptual shift from seeing your partner as a sex object (much like a sex toy) to seeing them as a sexual *person* endowed with intrinsic worth and dignity. This means that you respect your partner for their own sake, not merely for what they are willing and able to do in bed.

Kant (2004) expresses this view in terms of a "Categorical Imperative" (unconditional command) to always treat people, whether in your own person or that of another, as an "end in itself" and never as a "mere means" (sec. 2). Treating your partner as "an end in itself" means respecting their rational autonomy. If you manipulate or use your partner in this or that way, without their consent, inside or outside the bedroom, then you are treating them as a "mere means," not as an "end in itself"!

Speak Thou to your loved one and others in your life

This idea of treating another person as an end and not as a mere means receives an Eastern twist in the hands of philosopher Martin Buber (2011), who, as discussed in the introduction, eloquently speaks of two ways to address persons as well as objects. In our usual commerce with everyday affairs, we look at things as "It," that is, we analyze and assess them for the ways they enter into our lives from a practical perspective. Thus, I may consider the tree in my yard as a collection of properties—leaves, trunk, branches, a certain size, and expanse occupying specific spatial coordinates in my yard, blocking out the intense heat from the sun, and providing shade. I may, however, stop and behold the tree as something majestic. In this state of awe, I am captivated by the way it reaches toward the sky and grows luxuriantly out of the earth, connecting with the flora and fauna surrounding it, bowing before me as its branches sway in the wind, connecting me with it and it with me. In this panoply of interrelated existence, the tree is no longer a solitary existence in time and space but, instead, a Thou into which I and all else coalesce and become one unified universe.

Of course, when I turn from the tree to go about the affairs of my practical life, it returns to its status as "It." It may, in the latter state of mind, appear to me in need of trimming. I look upon its fallen leaves now, not as its way of unity with all else but rather as something that needs to be raked up and discarded.

So, we do not remain suspended in the I–Thou relationship with the tree (or any other object, natural or manufactured) but instead fluctuate, to one extent or another, between "I–It" and "I–Thou."

In a similar manner, one may relate to another human being as "It," such as when a physician looks at his patient as a case of stage 4 metastatic cancer. Indeed, to be a good physician, one needs to address the disease, its prognosis, and its treatment. However, a good physician needs also to see his patient as Thou. In this capacity, the patient is not his disease, not a case to be studied, not a medical problem to be addressed, not *merely* a patient. Indeed, the patient is still a patient. This is not subtracted. Instead, to be Thou, the patient emerges as a person, in unity with other persons. It occupies the intensive care unit, which is part of the larger hospital community, which is part of the healthcare system, and with all other persons outside the system, which includes all humanity. As such, the physician is no longer separated from the patient in time and space (the patient in bed, the physician at the bedside) but each is mutually joined together and with all else in the universe.

> Buber (2011) eloquently expresses this unity:
> If I face a human being as my Thou, and say the primary word I-Thou to him, he is not a thing among things, and does not consist of things.
>
> This human being is not He or She, bounded from every other He and She, a specific point in space and time within the net of the world; nor is he a nature able to be experienced and described, a loose bundle of named qualities. But with no neighbour, and whole in himself, he is Thou and fills the heavens. This does not mean that nothing exists except himself. But all else lives in his light (pt. 1, ch. 7).

In enduring romantic love, there should be no delusion that the practical "I–It" relationship evaporates into a continuous, unending "I–Thou" relationship. Lovers are invested in helping one another to cope with the vicissitudes of everyday life. So, there may be a financial problem; a parenting issue; a problem at work; the loss of a parent; and an illness. Partners who truly love each other tend to be there to work through such challenges together, cooperatively. Notice I said, "tend to be there," not "are always there" because human beings are not perfect, and being truly in love is no exception. Indeed, it is such fallibility that defines human relationships whether they be "I–It" or "I–Thou" relationships. In relating as Thou to your lover, you do not transcend your imperfections, nor does your lover transcend hers, but instead you mutually bring them to the relationship.

You have the incredible capacity to forge a life plan and to define yourself through it

Following Rene Descartes (see Chapter 2), according to the French existentialist philosopher, Jean-Paul Sartre (2007), human reality starts with affirmation of one's existence as demonstrated through one's own thinking. The more you think, the more self-aware you become. So, you are not like moss, fungus, or cauliflower—all of which lack consciousness. As a self-aware being, you have the incredible capacity to project yourself into the future to create a plan for yourself, by which you can build your future, and, thereby, define yourself. So, you are not like the computer earlier mentioned, which is produced with a purpose in mind. Instead, you have the capacity to create your own purpose by acting on a plan that you create for yourself. Sartre (2007) expresses this by saying that for human beings, unlike manufactured objects, "existence precedes essence" (p. 21). Hence, you are responsible for who you are and who you become.

Sartre is clear that we do not equally exercise our creative capacity to define ourselves through our life plans. Thus, you may tell yourself that you are not any good at forging a romantic relationship, and, thereby, choose to live as a single person. This is, indeed, your choice, and you are responsible for it. However, what is special about all of us is that we possess this creative power to consciously choose what we make of ourselves. "Our aim," states Sartre, "is exactly to establish the human kingdom as a set of values distinct from the material world," in other words, to distinguish human beings from mere objects that lack self-awareness (p. 41). This means that each of us enjoys the same special status in this "human kingdom." Thus, the respect you accord to yourself is also the respect you accord to others, and vice versa.

In an intimate relationship, our life plans through which we define one another overlap so that your partner's plan includes yours and yours includes theirs. Because you simply are your life plan, as actualized through your actions, who we are is indissolubly and seamlessly bound together. So, in intimacy, you become a part of me, and I become a part of you.

In bed, my sexual identity is bound up with you and mine with you. My sexual desires acted out in bed with you, and yours with me, become inseparable from our respective beings, hence intertwined with one another. My satisfactions are yours and mine yours since our sexual acts do not exist independently of one another. It is your body that is stimulated by my caress and mine by yours. When I think of who I am sexually, my identity includes you in the most intimate and personal ways. The knowledge you have of my body, and that I have of yours, distills in the very thought!

Outside the bedroom, my life and yours cross in myriad ways and I may not change my life without changing yours. If I take on a new job with longer hours, we may find that our routines change, which may, at least temporarily, alter the rhythm of settled ways. But in enduring love, there is unconditional respect for one's partner, even if the change is not welcome. This is because our subjective worlds are too intertwined to reject you without taking away an irreplaceable part of myself, and conversely. So, in true love, we tend to tolerate change. This does not mean that all change is acceptable; but there is, in any event, acceptance of you, and you of me. So, both inside the bedroom and outside it, building intimate relationships portends mutual, unconditional acceptance.

Stop clinging to your successes and accept your failures too

Buddhism also teaches unconditional acceptance of others as well as oneself (Ellis, 2005). This means that we should develop tolerance for ourselves and others even when we fail at things or when others treat us unkindly. No less than others, you have positive as well as negative qualities, that is, some that are desirable and others that are not. So, to accept yourself and others unconditionally means to accept yourself and others regardless of your or others' successes or failures, triumphs or defeats, desirable aspects or negative ones. For example, you may be successful professionally but not in your private life, having been divorced twice. Accepting yourself, unconditionally, means acknowledging *both* your successes and failures while refusing to rate yourself based on them.

Successes and failures are contingent, fleeting things. Sometimes we succeed, and other times we fail. Clinging to your successes leads to much anxiety since you will never be certain that your successes will last in the future. Likewise, others you exalt as great successes may meet similar fates, and thus shake the foundations of your respect. Such respect, based on the good qualities you or others possess, is very fragile, indeed, and contingent on good fate and bad. On the other hand, respect based on the person, as such, is unshakeable because it is constant regardless of successes or failures.

It is also by courageously acknowledging the negative aspects of ourselves and others that we can become better at things. Thus, you can use your mistakes and those of others as guides to doing better in the future. "I was so wrapped up in my work life that I didn't take seriously that I was neglecting my personal life, and now I am alone. So, I need to work harder in the future at balancing my work life with my personal life."

Let others, especially your enemies, help you to cultivate serenity by helping you to be more tolerant

The greatest lessons may also be learned from others, especially those whom you may regard as your enemies. According to the Dalai Lama (n.d.), our enemies

> are the ones who give us the most trouble, so if we truly wish to learn, we should consider enemies to be our best teacher!
>
> For a person who cherishes compassion and love, the practice of tolerance is essential, and for that, an enemy is indispensable. So, we should feel grateful to our enemies, for it is they who can best help us develop a tranquil mind! (sec. 6).

As such, Buddhism prescribes unconditional acceptance for everyone, even your enemies, who may turn out to be your greatest teachers. Indeed, how could you learn to be tolerant of others if no one ever tried your patience!

Cultivating tolerance in your interpersonal relationships is key to working through issues that will inevitably arise, even in very stable relationships. In intimate relationships, not everything your partner does will be copasetic, and you will need to tolerate their negative aspects along with their positive ones. So, they may, in your estimation, tend to be overly afraid of bad things happening and tend to worry more than you about them. In such cases, it may be like howling at the wind to get them to change. If you *demand* that they be more like you, this is likely to generate a good deal of anger. It is the latter anger that may be your biggest barrier to cultivating enduring love, and not your partner's tendency to worry more than you about things. Once you learn to be more tolerant of your partner's perceived negative aspects, you are more likely to avoid much needless stress, both inside and outside the bedroom.

Thus, your reassurance may work much better than displays of anger in helping your partner to relax more. A hug is much more likely to lead to a gratifying outcome than a scowl. The consolation you provide may be the interlude (and foreplay) to further acts of loving kindness, including making love!

As human beings, you and your beloved are very special; You are children of God

From a Judeo-Christian perspective, you may see yourself and others as children of God, and hence in possession of intrinsic worth and dignity. According to

Roman Catholic Saint Thomas Aquinas (2018), human beings participate, albeit imperfectly, in the Divine Intellect by virtue of being rational beings. While human reason is far inferior to that of God, it is the imprint of Divine Wisdom and thus adds meaning to the claim that God made humankind in his own image.

So, in relation to all other creatures in the universe, you and your partner are quite special, indeed, according to this philosophy. Unlike other creatures, you participate in God's Divine Plan by way of knowledge. Thus, not only do you live together cooperatively; but also know that it is good and right to do so. In bed, you do not simply come together for procreative purposes, as do other animals; you also know that this is good and right, and express this knowledge in terms of making love, not just having sex.

While the Thomistic philosophy proscribes recreational sex, or sex not aiming at procreation, this does not mean that nonprocreative sex is necessarily off limits to the deeply religious couple. For example, a couple could plan sex to avoid ovulation. Couples may be past the child-bearing age, or otherwise unable to conceive. Further, there is sanctity in making love, which transcends the mere animalistic tendency toward procreation. No other animals, save for human beings, are capable of such a spiritually uplifting experience, since it is not possible among beings that lack the Divine imprint of reason. So, making love, in a committed relationship, even if not for purposes of procreation, celebrates this sanctified union.

Seek moderation in your pleasures

This is not to degrade the sentient, nonrational side of humanity. As Aristotle (2009) clearly perceived, human beings are rational *animals*. If we were purely rational beings, lacking bodies, purely spiritual beings, love would not be *human* love. Saint Augustine (2018) remarked that "[f]or the corruptible body presseth down the soul, and the earthly tabernacle weigheth down the mind that museth upon many things" (bk.12, art.15). It is only by transcending bodily feelings that one can attain communion with the Divine.

However, in the commerce of everyday life on earth, human relationships (the relationships we have with other human beings) are infused with bodily impulses having both positive and negative hues. Like an artist's palate, such bodily feelings are sundry and varied. The taste and feel of wine on the palate are not the same as that of bread. The throbbing or pulsating in the genitalia during sex is *sui generis*. Such somatosensory feelings shape and form our experiences or perception of the world—the surrealistic experience of the birth of one's child; the thrill of getting your diploma or degree after so many years of persevering; the elation of landing your dream job; the relief felt when you find out that the tumor is benign. Intertwined are also negative feelings—the bittersweet retirement party; the gut-wrenching shock of learning that your partner has cheated on you; or the empathy you feel when hearing about the unfortunate plight of a friend. These feelings are not optional parts of our material existence here on earth, as though you could detach yourself from them without losing your humanity.

But this mixed set of intertwined, positively and negatively valent feelings can be allies in our dealings with the vicissitudes of life, or they can thwart such efforts. The feeling of contempt or disgust felt in your gut, when you feel betrayed, can lead you to act precipitously and regret it later. But the compassion you feel for the suffering of others can lead you to engage in charitable acts. The high of an intoxicating beverage can lower your inhibitions and lead you to act or say things you shouldn't have. But the danger alarm felt inside you can lead you to spring into action and save a loved one. *Cognitive dissonance* arises when you feel inclined to do something you know would be wrong—like permitting yourself to be seduced by your partner's "best friend."

A very wise ancient Greek philosopher, Epicurus (n.d.), admonished us against getting carried away by pleasant feelings to act in ways that are self-defeating—that is, bring more displeasure in the end. Yet he emphasized the importance of pleasure in attaining happiness. However, while the pleasures of good friends, the examined life, freedom or autonomy, and a balanced diet provide the ingredients of a happy life, other pleasures can be self-destructive. The latter include overindulgence or excess and caving to desires for immediate gratification without regard to long-term pleasures (maintaining a healthy lifestyle, for example).

Indeed, according to Epicurus, the secret to happiness lies in moderation in the seeking of pleasures and avoidance of pain. Avoiding the extremes is key. A glass of wine can, other things being equal, be good for digestion, but consuming the entire bottle is not only unhealthy but can impair perception and judgment.

From this Epicurean viewpoint, enduring love cannot work without regard to a life of moderate pleasures and the absence of pain. If you or your partner go to extremes, whether at the dinner table (overeating, for example) or in the bedroom (taking hallucinogens like Ecstasy to have sex), then you have likely crossed the lines of moderation countenanced by Epicurus. While a happy, loving relationship needs infusion with positive experiences and the absence of negative ones, it is likely to be defeated by the excesses of imbibing, too much or too little.

"My partner is boring" or "They're not fun" are vague personal attacks that can impede the unconditional acceptance of your partner. There are, indeed, reasonable limits to what can be packed into terms such as "fun" or "boring." If my partner doesn't like getting high, that doesn't mean they're "boring" or "not fun." Consuming psychoactive drugs or alcohol is not a condition of enduring love and may, and often does, destroy the prospect of attaining it when it leads to dependency or addiction. Discussing, with your partner, possible ways to increase positive experiences, or reduce negative ones, can demonstrate respect for your partner and the relationship. Degrading or disparaging them with personal attacks is counterproductive, and likely to create animosity and thwart the quest for happiness.

"Okay, but aren't some people really boring and not fun?" The obvious answer is, "Of course," but beware of "the obvious"! "I am bored by his repeatedly doing the same old things and rarely trying anything new" or "I don't have fun when we do these same old things" are acceptable ways to express a lack of contentment. These expressions are consistent with making constructive future changes. They do not involve off-putting personal attacks likely to breed further negative feelings.

In the bedroom, demonstrating unconditional acceptance of your partner follows suit. Exploring new ways to improve sexual arousal can be constructive. Thus, I do not have to accept the status quo to unconditionally accept my partner; for I do not have to accept what they say or do to accept *them*. "But what should I do if they are unwilling to try new things in bed to please me?"

Epicurus, again, reminds you not to throw away long-term satisfaction for immediate satisfaction. This entails not sabotaging a meaningful relationship because there are some negative aspects of it. Here, it is important to keep perspective. From an Epicurean perspective, this means weighing the negatives and positives of the relationship and striking a balance. Indeed, sabotaging the relationship, as it can be better, makes little sense. This is not to say that there are never cogent reasons to end a relationship. However, it is generally true that relationships that have a strong foundation in unconditional self and other acceptance are more likely to improve over time than ones that are based on the desire for immediate gratification.

> **Cultivating Respect in Romantic Love**
>
> In this video, I discuss the impediment of damnation to romantic love and the importance of respect to overcome it.
>
>
>
> https://youtu.be/eP-tDUUzyEE

Identifying Some Core Philosophical Aspects of Unconditional Acceptance of Self and Others

Here are some aspects of the philosophies discussed in this chapter that appear to be essential to overcoming the tendency to damn yourself and others; attain unconditional respect for self and others; and, thus, build intimacy in romantic love.

- As persons, you and your partner, are autonomous, self-determining agents. This means that neither you nor your partner are objects to be used and manipulated. When an object no longer serves its purpose, it is discarded. Persons are not objects to be discarded when they cease to serve some perceived purpose, whether inside or outside the bedroom.
- Whether in the bedroom or outside it, perceive the *whole person* of your partner as well as yourself as a being worthy of respect, without dissection into this or that weakness or pravity that blinds you from the whole. So, when you meet your partner, whether inside or outside the bedroom, meet them as a person. This means not as a flawless being but rather one whose flaws are seamlessly incorporated into the whole such that this specialness marks them out as a being to be cherished; and so too for yourself along with your own specialness.
- Neither you nor your partner are mere "Its" to be used *only* for this or that purpose. Today you need them to help you with a chore; tomorrow they help you; you work cooperatively, by mutual consent, not forced or deceived, but with mutuality and respect. Then tomorrow or tonight, as you caress each other, look

deeply into each other's eyes. See into that special person, not as an "It," but filled with the splendor of the whole being who is unique, not without the flaws that coalesce with their entire being, but the special person they truly are.

- You and your partner have this incredible attribute of subjectivity; unlike moss or cauliflower, you are a conscious, self-aware being who has this incredible capacity to project your life plan into the future. Who you are, or who you become, is a function of how you and your partner, respectively, define yourselves. In building a life in common, you define yourselves (partly) in a manner that intwines your existences. This coalescence through intertwining, interactive, mutually supportive self-definitions, or life plans, is a major part of what it means to forge an enduring, romantic love.
- Human beings are imperfect by their nature, so it is in vain to demand perfection in your partner, or yourself before you can be contented in your relationship.
- Holding out and refusing to change are also futile since nature is continuously changing, and you are part of nature. The greatest obstacle to constructive change lies in a lack of tolerance. Impatience that seeds anger and hostility only serves to thwart constructive change by shutting down the avenues for meaningful and respectful communication.
- Whether or not you are a religious person, there is, indeed, a spiritual aspect of enduring romantic love. For such love transcends mere carnal lust and its satisfaction. There is something transcendent, if not divine, about such mutual sharing of two human beings. In the bedroom, there is an ineffable presence of an elevated status beyond mere flesh—the spirituality of two bodies rhythmically communicating abstract meanings of "solidarity," "mutuality," "hopefulness," "faith," and "love." If you are religious, then these ideas reflect the infinite wisdom and goodness of the Divine mind. If you are agnostic or atheistic, you need not withhold belief in the deep meanings infusing such a marvelous experience. For, regardless of its source—whether a function of neural circuitry firing in harmonious interplay or something else—its inherent value is non-negotiable.
- This incredibly pleasurable experience is a dimension of the intrinsic value of romantic love, as distinct from just having sex. This value attached to an enduring love is founded on mutual unconditional respect. Without such appreciation for each other, as persons, the odds of forging deeply gratifying experiences both inside and outside the bedroom are not possible or diminish exponentially. This means distinguishing between accepting what your partner is doing (or not doing) and their value as a person. Thus, it is not *they* who aren't fun, or who are boring, although they may be *doing or refusing to do* something you find boring, or just not fun.

Applying the Eclectic Philosophy through Cognitive–Behavioral Practice

Applying these philosophical frames requires practice. This means using them to cultivate greater respect for yourself and your partner, as well as others. You can work toward this goal by doing the cognitive–behavioral exercises and applying the guidelines I have provided for building respect in your everyday life:

EXERCISE 1

Assessing Reciprocal Strengths and Weaknesses

Accepting each other unconditionally means that you avoid name-calling, putdowns, and global ratings based on certain attributes you think are negative (for example, "a boring person"). Instead, it is helpful to stick to judgments about specific attributes you like about your partner and ones you may want your partner to work on. This activity is intended to help you and your partner practice framing your perspectives about each other in the latter more constructive manner.

1. Write down what you take to be the strengths (positives) of your partner as they relate to your relationship (for example, helps with domestic chores, honest, caring). Then write down what you take to be the weaknesses (for example, does not like to try different things in bed, talks about self too much). What things do you like best? What things do you like least?
2. Ask your partner to prepare similar lists, and identify things liked best and least.

Sit down with your partner to discuss your respective lists. Start by taking turns, sharing your list of strengths and the ones you like best. Then, do the same for weaknesses.

3. Brainstorm about what things you each would be prepared to work on changing.
4. Going forward, practice your respective changes during your daily lives together.

> **EXERCISE 2**
>
> **Shame-Attacking Exercise**
>
> This activity can help you work on unconditional self-acceptance. Many people base their self-worth on what others think about them. The goal of this exercise is to practice accepting yourself, even if you think that others disapprove of you in some way. Keep in mind that unconditional self-acceptance is a condition of unconditional acceptance of others, which, in turn, is a condition of enduring, romantic love.
>
> 1. Stage an event in which you do something embarrassing or shameful to you. For example, this may be (deliberately) making a "dumb mistake" in front of others. It may be wearing clothing that you would be embarrassed to wear, doing something humiliating like buying only Pepto Bismol at a grocery store and burping or farting while checking out, eating by yourself in a restaurant, or any other (harmless) thing, of your choosing, that would embarrass you.
> 2. After staging this event, work through your self-doubts. So, others think there's something wrong with you; but so what? Does that really change who you are as a person? Does that lower your self-worth? What would the Buddhists tell you? What would Kant say? What would Sartre say? What about Buber?" In working through your embarrassment, use any philosophies, of your choosing, that resonate with you, in working through your self-doubts.

Guidelines for building respect for yourself and your partner as well as others

- Treat your partner, as well as other people, including yourself, as autonomous beings. In the bedroom, this means not forcing, deceiving, threatening, or otherwise manipulating your partner into doing what you want, against his will. Conversely, don't allow *yourself* to be treated similarly by your partner. So, your partner demonstrates his lack of respect for you by attempting to threaten you into obedience. "I'm breaking up if you won't let me bind you to the bed posts." Here would be a good time to show your partner (and yourself) that you have unconditional self-respect by refusing to allow yourself to be forced into subservience. "I feel disrespected by you when

you try to force me to do things that I don't feel comfortable doing. This is not going to work if our relationship is based on manipulation and threats instead of mutual respect."
- Do not use derogatory, degrading labels or attributions when you have disagreements with your partner. "You are stupid" or "There must be something wrong with you" are locutions that should not be uttered.
- Do not say that your partner is "boring," or "not fun," or launch any similar personal attacks on her. Instead, speak about what you would like them to do differently, keeping in mind that it is their behavior, not *themselves*, you have an issue with.
- Consider the positives and negatives of the relationship instead of focusing on just one aspect of it. (See the first featured activity in this chapter.)
- As you and your partner age, you will inevitably change, including how you both perceive reality; so, embrace change, rather than dogmatically refusing to change. You can embrace change by being open to making changes, especially ones that have the potential to lead to further constructive changes. For example, your partner asks you to listen more and be less self-defensive. In the end, by refusing to change accordingly you affect change anyway, albeit negative change—your partner is less contented than they otherwise would be. However, in working to change, you affect positive change that may spark further change. Thus, your partner may become more open to making constructive changes you want them to make. This is how couples grow together and become more interconnected over time.
- Seek long-term satisfaction rather than caving to immediate gratification that scuttles long-term happiness. This is possible to the extent that you avoid the extremes in seeking pleasure and avoiding pain. This requires exercising willpower and self-control. "I really find my secretary to be sexy but having an affair with them would be utterly disrespectful and hurtful to my partner and would defeat our mutual, long-term happiness in the end. I will be candid with them that I am in a committed relationship."
- Enjoying each other does not require adornments and luxury. Thus, dining at a moderately priced restaurant or having an intimate, candlelight dinner for two at home can be just as pleasurable as dining at an expensive restaurant. You also do not need to wait for a special occasion to enjoy yourselves. For example, take an evening walk together, savor the time together, live in the here and now without discussing unpleasantries; hold hands, gently kiss; soak up the scenery, smile, and laugh together!
- Seek spirituality in relating to your partner both inside and outside the bedroom, whether, or not, you are religious. Cognitively reframe your

relationship as having a transcendent character. This can set the climate for openness to deeper and deeper levels of intimacy that would be lost by perceiving your relationship and its intimate character merely as a product of physical exchanges defined in terms of hormones.

In the above ways, you can begin to build and practice a behavior plan for increasing unconditional self and other acceptance. Cultivating the core aspects of the eclectic philosophy assembled here can help you to overcome self- and other damning tendencies that impede the progress toward an enduring romantic love by helping to support increased unconditional self- and other acceptance.

Keep in mind, as well, that the latter virtues are not merely reserved for the bedroom, the dinner table, or the family affair. Indeed, practicing such philosophies in your commerce with others outside the relationship as well as inside it—at the office, in dealing with the clerk at the grocery store, with friends, other relatives, etc.—is crucial. This is because human beings, all of them, are not objects to be used simply for this or that purpose. As emphasized here, they are special beings with conscious life, rationality, autonomy, life plans, and the incredible capacity for transcending the mundane aspects of material existence in forging relationships.

So, trying to separate your relationship with your partner from all other human relationships is artificial and self-defeating; for in lack of respect for others outside the relationship, you merely prime yourself to treat your partner in the same manner. Lovers are not merely lovers inside their loving relationships; they are loving and caring people outside too. This does not entail the absurd conclusion that you should practice sexual intimacy with others outside your relationship. It is rather to say that the ideas of unconditional self and other acceptance and their supportive philosophies as presented here are also antidotes to self- and other-damning tendencies that extend to others outside the relationship. Thus, much work lies ahead, but you now have the cognitive-emotive machinery to make admirable progress toward attaining an enduring romantic love.

References

Aristotle. 2009. *Politics*. The Internet Classics Archive. http://classics.mit.edu//Aristotle/politics.html.

Allport, Gordon. 1979. *The Nature of Prejudice*. New York: Basic Books.

Aquinas, Thomas. 2018. *Summa Theologica*, trans. Frs. of the English Dominican Province. Claremont, CA: Coyote Canyon Press.

Augustine, Aurelius. 2014. *The City of God*, Vol. 1, trans. M. Dodds. Project Gutenberg Ebook. https://www.gutenberg.org/files/45304/45304-h/45304-h.htm.

Bandura, Albert. 1990. "Mechanisms of Moral Disengagement." In *Origins of Terrorism: Psychologies, Ideologies, Theologies, States of Mind*, ed. by Walter Reich, 161–191, Washington, DC: Woodrow Wilson Center Press.

Berne, Eric. 1964. *Games People Play: The Basic Handbook of Transactional Analysis*. New York: Ballantine Books.

Buber, Martin. 2011. *I and Thou*, trans. R. G. Smith & T.&T. Clark. Internet Archives https://archive.org/details/IAndThou_572/mode/2up.

Cohen, Elliot D. 2022. June 9. "Do You Have Imposter Syndrome? How to Identify and Overcome It with Logic-Based Therapy. Psychology Today. https://www.psychologytoday.com/us/blog/what-would-aristotle-do/202206/do-you-have-imposter-syndrome.

Dalai Lama & Cutler, Howard C. 2009. *The Art of Happiness*. New York: Penguin Publishing Group (Kindle ed.). https://www.amazon.com/Art-Happiness-10th-Anniversary-Handbook-ebook/dp/B002UK6NO0.

Dalai Lama. n.d. "Compassion and the Individual." His Holiness: The 14th Dalai Lama of Tibet. https://www.dalailama.com/messages/compassion-and-human-values/compassion.

Ellis, Albert. 2001. *Overcoming Destructive Beliefs, Feelings, and Behaviors: New Directions for Rational Emotive Behavior Therapy*. Ithaca, NY: Prometheus Books.

Ellis, Albert. 2005. *The Myth of Self-Esteem: How Rational Emotive Behavior Therapy Can Change Your Life Forever*. Ithaca, NY: Prometheus Books (Kindle ed.). https://www.amazon.com/Myth-Self-esteem-Rational-Emotive-Behavior-ebook/dp/B003N647B6.

Epicurus. n.d. *Letter to Menoeceus*, trans. Robert Drew Hicks. Internet Classics Archive. http://classics.mit.edu/Epicurus/menoec.html.

Fromm, Erich. 2006. *The Art of Loving*. New York: Harper Collins.

Gepp, Karin & Lebow, Hilary I. 2022, September 6. "What Are the Signs of a Victim Mentality?" Psych Central. https://psychcentral.com/health/victim-mentality.

Gills, Kaytee. 2022, February 19. "10 Ways Childhood Trauma Can Manifest in Adult Relationships." Psychology Today. https://www.psychologytoday.com/us/blog/invisible-bruises/202202/10-ways-childhood-trauma-can-manifest-in-adult-relationships.

Kant, Immanuel. 2004. *Fundamental Principles of The Metaphysics of Morals*, trans. Thomas Kingmill Abbott. Project Gutenberg E-book. https://www.gutenberg.org/files/5682/5682-h/5682-h.htm.

Lünnemann, M. K. M., Van der Horst, F. C. P., Prinzie, P., Luijk, M. P. C. M., & Steketee, M. 2019. "The Intergenerational Impact of Trauma and Family Violence on Parents and Their Children." *Child Abuse & Neglect*, 96: 104–134. https://doi.org/10.1016/j.chiabu.2019.104134.

Pereira, A., Santos, J. P., Sardinha, P., Cardoso, J., Ramos, C., & Almeida, T. 2021. "The Impact of Childhood Abuse on Adult Self-Esteem and Emotional Regulation." *Annals of Medicine*, 53 (Suppl 1): S126. https://doi.org/10.1080/07853890.2021.1896171.

Plotinus. 1956. *Plotinus: The Enneads*, trans. Stephen MacKenna. London: Faber & Faber, Ltd.

Rogers, C. R. 1995. *On Becoming a Person: A Therapist's View of Psychotherapy*. New York: Harper One.

Sartre, Jean-Paul. 2007. *Existentialism is a Humanism*, trans. Carol Macomber. Yale University Press (Kindle ed.). https://www.amazon.com/Existentialism-Humanism-Jean-Paul-Sartre/dp/0300115466.

Yalom, Irvin D. & Leszcz, Molyn. 2020. *The Theory and Practice of Group Psychotherapy*. New York: Basic Books.

CHAPTER 4

BUILDING SELF-CONTROL IN ROMANTIC LOVE

> Impulsive partners wreck their relationships with their thoughtless misdeeds, while those with self-control hold their urges in check and keep their eye on the long-term.
>
> —David Ludden, *Psychology Today*

Poor Self-Control as an Impediment

As you have seen, enduring love requires nurturing. This means having patience. Unfortunately, many relationships fail in achieving such a love due to poor self-control. Metaphorically put, this means having a low boiling point. Suppose your partner goes shopping and leaves bags of groceries on the kitchen counter without putting them away. You arrive home two hours later to find the ice cream still in the grocery bag but by this time, it has melted and made a chocolaty mess. You see it and lose control. Raising your voice, you summon your partner to the scene of the perceived crime, and declare, "How could you do such a stupid thing! Don't you know you're supposed to put the groceries away!?"

Of course, you are only human, and it is understandable how a person could get upset about this, especially if you were looking forward to chocolate ice cream for dessert! However, there is a big difference between "understandable" and "justified" or "warranted." The latter terms ("justified" or "warranted") refer to whether your anger is rational, that is, whether you have a good reason to be angry. The former term ("understandable") refers to whether your response can be explained by a set of facts that led to the response. So, to say that your response is understandable is not necessarily to say that it is justified or warranted. Let the person who has never forgotten to do a simple chore cast the first stone!

Indeed, it is inevitable that, in sharing your life with another human being, you will encounter many instances where what you think *should* be, and what *is*, do not coincide. So, if your tendency is to lose your cool in such everyday situations, you are likely to spend a good part of your relationship on a collision course. Unfortunately, this is not the way you are likely to build an enduring, romantic love.

In connection with this major bulwark to enduring love (poor self-control), I have often spoken, metaphorically, about a willpower muscle. This is the internal muscle that allows you to control how you respond to situations you perceive to be challenging. It is the internal sense of power you perceive when you feel an inclination to go in one direction while at the same time, feeling an opposing force. So, you might feel inclined to "tell your partner off" while at the same time, feeling a force opposing this. If, despite this opposite force, the reprimanding words "What a dumbass thing to do!" burst from your lips, you experience weakness of the will.

Your willpower, however, can be directed by practical reasoning. Practical reasoning is reasoning whose conclusion prescribes or evaluates something. "It is wrong to lie to my partner. Telling her that I was at work when I was really having beer with the guys, would be a lie. So, it would be wrong for me to tell her this." Thus, even if you feel inclined to lie, to cover up a misdeed, you may exercise your willpower to tell the truth, nevertheless. On the other hand, if you have a weak willpower muscle, you may cave to your inclination to lie.

When you know that something would be wrong, but your feelings (emotions or desires) pull you in the opposite direction, you are in a state of what psychologists call *cognitive dissonance*. Being in such a state of conflict can be a good thing because you, at least, know right from wrong, and therefore possess the wisdom to act according to your considered judgment. As such, it is a matter of strengthening your willpower muscle so that when you encounter cognitive dissonance (as you, inevitably, will in everyday life), you can exercise your willpower muscle on the side of doing what you perceive to be the right thing.

There are four different types of perceived loss of control, over which you can exercise your willpower muscle. Perceived inability to:

1. *do* things that involve risk-taking.
2. control your *emotions*.
3. tolerate other people or things that are *frustrating*.
4. control unwanted, intrusive *thoughts*.

In each of these cases, human beings *can't*stipate themselves, that is, irrationally convince themselves that they *can't* control or manage their behavior, emotions, frustrations, or cognitions (thoughts) (Cohen, 2022). First, you may *feel*, at a gut level, a sense of inertia or disempowerment, which you then express using the little words, "I can't" (or their equivalent) to disavow freedom and responsibility to control yourself.

However, accepting the freedom and responsibility to control yourself is a precondition to overcoming your perceived loss of control. If you tell yourself that you *can't* control yourself, then you probably *won't*. Table 4.1 sums up each of these types of *can't*stipation. In this chapter, I look carefully at each of them.

Table 4.1 T.ypes of *can't*stipation

Type of Can'tstipation	Definition	Self-Defeating Result	Example
1. Behavioral	Telling yourself that you *can't do* certain things that you really can do but choose not to do.	Sustains or creates self-defeating behavior	"I can't make a commitment because what if it didn't work out."
2. Emotional	Instead of taking responsibility for your emotions, blaming them on external events; thus telling yourself you have *no control* over them.	Sustains self-defeating emotions and blocks self-control.	"I can't help feeling anxious about my performance during sex."
3. Frustration	Telling yourself that you can't stand or tolerate certain things or people when you find them to be frustrating.	Sustains low frustration tolerance. You seek immediate gratification and give up or lose patience.	"I can't stand to wait, so I don't do anything that takes a lot of time."
4. Cognitive	Telling yourself that you can't get a certain "bad thought" out of your mind.	Sustains self-defeating thoughts	"I can't get that thought out of my head about something terrible happening to my partner."

Behavioral can'tstipation

Telling yourself you can't control your behavior can be a major problem for achieving a lasting love life, both inside and outside the bedroom. Perhaps you are experiencing anxiety about having sex with your partner. "What if I don't get hard!" Consequently, you make excuses for not having sex ("I'm just too tired tonight"), thus resisting your partner's overtures. So, when you do finally have it, your rumination about the possibility of not having an erection places a strain on your performance. Hence, self-defeatingly, you bring about just what you feared in the first place!

In such cases, the root of the problem often lies in a *perfectionistic demand for certainty*. "I must be certain that I will have an erection; but, quite clearly, I am not certain; so, horror of horrors, I could fail to have an erection. And then what would my partner think of me! So, I just can't do it."

There is this deep visceral, *felt need* for certainty about having an erection that drives your anxiety about sleeping with your partner. But this feeling is just that, a feeling in your head. It does not point to the existence of a law of nature according to which you must be certain about the outcome of your sexual encounters. For, nowhere is it written that you must have such reassurance before you have sex. In fact, no human being has any such certainty. Indeed, if we had to be certain about the consequences of any action, before doing it, we would do nothing whatsoever. Thus, we venture out into the world with reasonable hopes and expectations that things will work out, and this is generally enough to keep us actively engaged in giving meaning to our lives. This is equally true outside the bedroom—at work or in social contexts—as it is in one's sex life.

Are you willing to try new and different things with your partner? Do you welcome having new adventures in life? Indeed, this involves taking some risks; for risks are the stuff of change. Take no risks and you suffer the peril of a humdrum universe that still encounters risks, especially those associated with stagnation and loss of vitality in your relationship. Enduring love flourishes with the taking of risks, albeit reasonable ones. So, there is a calculation in risk-taking. You ought not to jump out of a plane without a parachute and merely trust the wind that it will land you safely on the ground. But owing to your rational faculty, you can discern the reasonable from the unreasonable in planning your lives in common. There is, here, an ethics of risk. Some couples have a more liberal ethics of risk and prefer to take more substantial risks; others are more conservative and prefer taking fewer risks. But there are extremes that defy any sensible ethics of risk. The partner who refuses to take rational risks to forge a relationship, inside and outside the bedroom, is not likely to forge an enduring love.

Risk-taking is, of course, negotiable between partners. There is compromise. So, maybe we won't go skydiving, but we can go boating. Refusal to negotiate— "It's my way or the highway"—is not likely to end well. Here is where the cultivation of courage becomes important in the forging of enduring, romantic love. As Aristotle (1941) surmised, long ago, courage involves taking rational risks, which involves facing danger rationally. This means avoiding going to extremes. Cowardice is one extreme, rashness the other. "With regard to feelings of fear and confidence," spoke Aristotle, "courage is the mean; of the people who exceed, he who exceeds in fearlessness has no name (many of the states have no name), while the man who exceeds in confidence is rash, and he who exceeds in fear and falls short in confidence is a coward" (bk. 2, ch. 7).

Partners who are prepared to explore new and different ways of enhancing their relationship within such rational parameters, who have the courage to satisfy one another in a mutually considerate manner, have no need to be certain about the outcome of their experiences. Quite the contrary, they embark on adventures in living where the journey is jointly reassuring; where there is joy in seeing the other engaged in life, being guided by a sense of mutuality in growing together through such experiences in common. So, your spouse has never been to Paris and would love to shop on the Avenue des Champs-Élysées. This may not be your cup of tea, preferring a visit to a quaint British pub in London, instead. But you both would enjoy European travel. Perhaps you both would enjoy a visit to the Musée du Louvre. So, your itinerary could include all these attractions.

The excitement then lies in the travel together, as one, soaking up the scenes, as though the sensory organs of one partner were that of the other, thus nourishing each other, seamlessly. My joy is yours, and that of yours is mine; seeing the expression on your face excites me; and that on mine excites you. It is the foreplay leading to a romantic, candlelight dinner in a Parisian restaurant, wining and dining, as excitement crescendos in the hotel suite, reaching a climax in orgasmic sexual unity. This is where the union that began earlier in the day is now fully actualized in bed.

In this scenario, there is no place for demanding certainty; for this is only to eviscerate the point of the rendezvous. Indeed, in this saga, chance is not an intruder but rather a tour guide. For, whatever happens is a growth experience that transcends each of us, singly; whatever happens is an affirmation of the unitary, joint venture; the essence and core of what makes it an adventure.

So, the wine spills on the tablecloth, needing to be blotted up. A bit gently drips onto your suit pants leaving a red stain. This stain now commemorates the journey together. That precious evening in Paris when we later made love.

It is no longer a stain but a monument to love, embracing the uncertainty upon which this momentous occasion was founded. It is not this precious chance of the spilling of wine, the droplet embedded for eternity on your suit pants, that should be traded for certainty; for the latter is boring, sterile, routine, and devoid of excitement. Chance is to be rejoiced; for it signifies the chance to grow together in unity, through both the planned and unplanned, the predicted and unpredicted, and the fortunate and unfortunate. It is this theme and variation in the rhythm of life that finds its own mode of expression through such improvisation. Amid this glorious uncertainty, with its opportunities for constructive change, the antidote to stagnation, due to behavioral *can'tstipation*, is the cultivation of greater *decisiveness* to pursue life opportunities, and the *courage* to take the risks associated with them. (These virtues are examined later in this chapter.)

Emotional can'tstipation

How often have you told yourself (or at least assumed) that you couldn't control your emotions, blaming them instead on external events or people. "You made me angry by not telling me you were coming home late"; "You made me feel depressed when you didn't even notice my new outfit"; "My new job is causing me a lot of anxiety"; and "My financial situation is depressing me." These utterances seem so innocent. Isn't it understandable for you to get angry when your partner doesn't even call to say they were coming home late when you were expecting them? Isn't it only natural to feel down about not even noticing your new outfit despite that you were excited about seeing your partner's reaction, or about your dwindling savings account; or to experience anxiety in, say, the first couple weeks of a new job?

The answer to all these questions is a resounding YES! But to say so does not mean that you are simply a passive recipient of your emotions. There you are, minding your own business when someone or something comes along and causes you anguish. This is very simple. The problem is that it is too simple. First, there is a difference between what you are upset about, and what causes you to be upset. So, you may understandably be upset about your partner not calling to let you know they were coming home late. However, the event of your partner not calling you is not what caused you to be upset. What if you simply missed the call and were upset about your partner not calling. Indeed, the event of your partner not calling you would not even be true in this case. Yet, you might still be upset about them not calling you. "Oh, but then I would be upset because I *thought* they didn't call." Correct! It is your thoughts *about* external events that cause you to be upset, not the external events themselves.

In the human organism, the processing of thoughts is intimately bound up with emotions. Indeed, some neuropsychologists have convincingly argued that the same processes that control practical reasoning, that is, decision-making, are also involved in emotions (Damasio, 1994). Indeed, when I decide to book a flight to Paris, there is a positive feeling that pushes me in this direction; and there is likely a negative feeling that pulls me in the opposite direction if I decide not to book the flight. No number of facts, heaped upon themselves, can move me to act unless I feel so disposed. Thus, that I will get wet if I don't take an umbrella, will not ordinarily move to take the umbrella if I don't care about getting wet, or enjoy it. Of course, we may do things that we do not want to do. For example, I may force myself to take my yearly physical exam. But even here, there is a desire, or a feeling of obligation (yes, obligations are *felt* in a visceral sense too) to take care of myself. As such, human action and emotion are intimately bound up with one another in the practical sphere of living.

But not all feelings move us to act in constructive ways, and some may be extremely destructive. Rage may move you to do something that you end up regretting. Sadly, the prisons are filled with people who, due to surges of uncontrolled passion, end up performing regrettable acts—anything from assault and battery to murder.

Emotional *can't*stipation arises when you deny your ability to control your emotions. You tell yourself that you *can't* help your feelings, which, in turn, moves you to do or say what you end up regretting. "I can't help my feelings" is popularly stated, even when there is no good reason to think that you really *can't*. The latter means that you lack the *capacity* to control your feelings, that they somehow take control of you and drive you to act in self-destructive ways. Easy enough to say, right? Easy to make excuses. Much harder to exercise your willpower muscle!

This is not to say that there are no cases in which a brain lesion prevents someone from overriding a destructive or self-defeating emotion. It is rather to say that this is not the neurological basis for most cases of failure to control such emotions. It's an excuse, not a scientifically defensible explanation for failing to exercise self-control.

How many times in your relationship with your partner have you apologized for saying or doing something regrettable? Please don't apologize if you really *couldn't* do otherwise. For what would an apology even mean if you had no free will; no capacity to abstain from saying or doing the regrettable act? It would be like asking a tornado to apologize for the damage it has caused. The tornado truly has no power over its winds. But the destructive winds of human emotion are not like those of tornados; they are within our control. It is only by claiming that you can't control them that you give yourself a free pass *not* to control them.

This does not mean that you don't have to practice exercising control over your emotions to get better at it. Indeed, it does take practice; but this does not mean that you don't have the *capacity* to control your emotions. For this would be like saying that you don't have the capacity to play a certain chord on the guitar simply because you have not practiced it. If you didn't have the capacity, why bother practicing!

Exchanges of unbridled emotion among couples can and do get ugly. They taint the headwaters of building intimate and enduring love. In some cases, the couples kiss and make up, but in many cases, the stench of things said in anger does not easily fade and sets the stage for the next emotional outburst. Such a relationship suffers. It suffers in the bedroom because the tender embrace is overdue; and when, and if, it does happen, the relationship is strained. The titillations of sex help to temporarily hide the odor, like an air freshener covering up a foul odor. But the scent is still there; and with each successive emotional debasing, it becomes more pungent when the two partners come up for air. Such sex is not the intimacy of enduring love, although it may be passionate. Such passion may release negative energy; hostility is sublimated. The couple may make peace only to fall back into the same routine, leaving little opportunity for consistent cultivation of enduring love. Not until the couple takes hold of its *can't*stipated emotions can it begin the journey toward deeper intimacy and tenderness that unites two souls seamlessly and boundlessly in a harmonious relationship.

Outside the bedroom, this harmonious relationship manifests itself in respectfully working through conflicts. So, maybe you feel that your partner is spending too much time at work and not enough time with you. This need not spark angry outbursts and shouting matches. Rather, it may be the occasion for empathetic resonance. "I can see how you feel that way. On those nights when I'm working late, you are alone. It must be very lonely." Here, getting in touch with your partner's feelings of loneliness, and letting them know, may be more important than the actual solution, although the latter may be more readily found when these feelings are appreciated. What is counterproductive is one or both partners' refusal to take responsibility for their own unbridled outbursts of anger ("I can't control myself") instead of mutual, empathetic listening and understanding.

Frustration **can'tstipation**

Do you have *low frustration tolerance*? This means telling yourself that you can't stand people or things when they are frustrating. "I can't stand your constant complaining"; "I can't stand it when I don't perform well in bed"; "I can't stand it when you take so long to get ready." Here, you tell yourself that you do not have the capacity to tolerate things you don't like; make mistakes perform subpar; or wait to get what you want. So, you may suffer from *short-term hedonism*, which means that you demand immediate gratification. So, when you don't get it, you give up, throw a tantrum; or otherwise defeat your purposes by destroying your chance for long-term satisfaction. You may also not try new things because you think you might fail at them, which you tell yourself you couldn't stand; or you may make yourself depressed when you do poorly at something or fail at it.

Clearly, a relationship based on a habit of *low frustration tolerance* is bound to destroy the prospects for an enduring, romantic love. In the bedroom, such a relationship is dampened by stress, which manifests itself in reduced ability to have an orgasm or erection. Outside the bedroom, it can lead you to give up on advancing your career goals, leaving you frustrated, which you may take out on your partner, a potential "soft target" for displacing your frustration. You may, needlessly, get upset with your partner if they do not do what you want them to do when you want them to do it. Your partner may, in turn, feel controlled and nonautonomous. While no relationship is completely devoid of needless stress and frustration (after all, we are all human), a steady diet of such tension leads to a dysfunctional relationship. Thus, new healthier habits of relating to one's partner, to others, and to the world are requisite to forging a lasting, romantic love. Such healthy relating entails the cultivation of the virtues of self-control, including patience and perseverance. (These two virtues will be discussed later in this chapter.)

Cognitive can'tstipation

Are you afraid to entertain certain thoughts, so much so that your life has little room for anything else but your futile attempts to escape them? "I can't stand the thought of my doing something horrible to my partner." Thus, you may imagine yourself bludgeoning them to death and then become inundated with self-doubt. "If I really love them, why did I have this horrible thought? I just can't stop thinking about it! What kind of monster would even have such a thought!?" And the more you try to get rid of the thought, the more it raises its ugly head in your mind. In an intimate moment with your lover, there it is again, conjuring up self-doubt, poisoning the moment, making it hard to love; becoming the failure that the thought says you are. However, the artist who has created this colossal nightmare is YOU. You are Dr. Frankenstein, and it is your monster, and only you can bury it. But, like Freddie Kruger, the fictional demon from the horror flick, *Nightmare on Elm Street*, the more you are afraid, the more real it becomes.

To the extent that this fear seriously disrupts your life on an ongoing basis, you may have a mental disorder known as obsessive-compulsive disorder (OCD), which can benefit from the care of a psychologist. So, what is said here is not, in that case, a substitute for therapy from a professional. However, because it can present such a strong impediment to enduring, romantic love, it should not go unexamined here.

There are two types of obsessions (1) moral and (2) existential. Moral obsessions involve having unwanted or intrusive thoughts that your "superego" (moral conscience) condemns, such as that of bludgeoning your lover to death. This type of obsession creates self-defeating, intense guilt for having even entertained the thought. Existential obsessions, on the other hand, involve having unwanted or intrusive thoughts about something bad happening to yourself or a loved one. Thus, you might imagine your lover dying of an infectious disease and, as a result, placing self-defeating restrictions on living a satisfactory life together. A relationship circumscribed by one or both forms of obsessiveness is unlikely to promote an enduring, romantic love. In fact, the likelihood is that the relationship will either end or drone on in a purgatory-like way until the problem is satisfactorily addressed through therapy.

The thinking that propels this obstacle to happiness forms an identifiable pattern. You tell yourself that you must be certain you would never do anything to (seriously) harm your loved one (moral obsessiveness) or that something very bad must never happen to your loved one (existential obsessiveness). However, you imagine yourself doing something horrible to your partner, or something horrible happening to them. So, you conclude that it's *not certain* you won't do it, or it won't happen. So, you think that you could *possibly* do it, which would make you a horrible person, or that the horrible thing in question might *really* happen. So, you tell yourself that *you can't stop thinking about it until you are certain it's not true*. As a result, your thinking turns into a vicious cycle, *ad nauseam*, thereby poisoning your waking hours with obsessive savoring of the unsavory and its attendant misery, because you keep checking to see if it's really true. To stop checking would be to leave yourself in a state of uncertainty, but this, you tell yourself, you must not do; so, on and on you go, until you have devoured your opportunity for a satisfactory life with your partner, both inside and outside the bedroom.

Overwhelmed by guilt or fear, you are distracted from life. Your partner, who may not be obsessive, is confused and frustrated. You may be ashamed to tell them what is going on inside your mind, especially in the case of moral obsessions, so you may become consumed by guilt, and it feels like it is tearing you apart inside. So, you may try to distract yourself from the thought, and it may seem to help a bit. However, there it is, ominously lurking in the background, threatening to raise its ugly head again and again, and thus you continue to live under its tyranny. Indeed, this has the potential to wreck an entire lifetime since the same obsession may continue, and/or another may take its place with no relief in sight until you make up your mind to do something about it!

As you will see, the key to getting rid of this vicious cycle of obsessive thinking and its destructive effect on the prospect of an enduring, romantic love, is the cultivation of three virtues: unconditional self-acceptance, unconditional life acceptance, and serenity.

Self-Control in Romantic Love

In this video, I discuss self-control as a key factor in building romantic love and the various virtues involved in cultivating self-control.

https://youtu.be/B5f5Uxbc9pY

Identifying the Virtues of Self-Control as Counters to *Can'tstipation*

Romantic lovers love themselves as they love each other. Perceiving life as a wonderous adventure, they courageously confront its inherent risks. There is, too, a deep serenity or peacefulness with which they greet each day of life together. Not easily discouraged from pursuing their goals, both collectively and individually, they are adeptly aware that progress toward attaining them takes time and patience.

The emotions of lovers harmonize, both consonantly and dissonantly, keeping time, with the rhythms of life, as fluctuations of fortune and misfortune rise and fall like the ocean tide. There is, thus, an appropriate emotion to accommodate the changing tide, from rapture to ennui, but neither mania nor depression.

Of course, this description is the ideal; that to which romantic lovers aspire. Veritably, they are not gods; they are flesh and blood and do not always act, think, and feel in the ways they know they should. Nor do they perform perfectly, without a hitch. Failure to reach a climax is not incompatible with the life of a lover. It matters how the matter is perceived. The courageous lover is not devastated, even if disappointed. The union is not dissolved, and the future is still open.

*Can'ts*tipated partners, on the other hand, may become depressed. Overcome by anxiety, they may fulfill their own prophecy. Guilt, anger, frustration, and regret thwart the potential for expressions of love. It is thus the virtues of self-control that hold the key to turning such a relationship around. The process is an ever-evolving one, not one that arises full-blown and complete in any given expanse of finite time. No matter how prosperous a relationship may be, there is always room for growth. Like a fine virtuoso who continues to improve, you may always find new opportunities to excel.

Overcoming cognitive can'tstipation through cultivating unconditional self- and life-acceptance, and serenity

If you have moral obsessions, it is likely that you struggle with issues of low self-esteem that adversely affect your relationship. Enduring lovers love themselves as they love each other. This means accepting oneself, unconditionally, as worthy of loving and being loved. This, in turn, means being comfortable with one's imperfections, and realizing that no human being is or can be perfect. The bad thoughts you entertain are powerless over you when you can affirm your self-worth, regardless of what thoughts enter your mind. Like a phantom, the hold that the thought has over you evaporates as you call it a bluff. "What kind of monster would have such a thought!" chides that inner demon. If you allow yourself to go down this rabbit hole, you will be suspended in self-doubt, checking, *ad nauseam*, to see if this thought demon is real. "I can't stop thinking about this ugly thought," you tell yourself in desperation.

Unconditionally self-accepting people refuse to play this sinister game, seeing through it, calling it the sham it truly is. As such, they can let the thoughts pass freely in and out of their minds. In this way, they attain serenity or peace of mind.

"I don't have to try to control these thoughts because they cannot harm me. Let them come and go as they please, it is no matter to me." An incredible weight is lifted, allowing you to devote your time to building an enduring love with your partner, instead of enslaving yourself to a false sense of incapacity to control your thoughts. Paradoxically, it is by not attempting to control these intrusive, unwanted thoughts that you can regain your freedom!

It is much the same in the case of existential obsessions. If you are having obsessive thoughts about something bad happening to your loved one, then your worry and fear are likely putting a damper on your relationship. Your partner is not likely to take your obsession as a sign of deep love for them, but rather feel as though you are destroying the chance to enjoy life. They are likely to feel like they are being dragged unwillingly through a series of dark tunnels with occasional glimmers of light at the end, only to be submerged in more darkness.

In contrast, one who has *unconditional life acceptance* does not perceive life as a series of dark tunnels with occasional light. Nor are they unrealistically optimistic about the challenges of living. Of course, shit happens, but so do wonderful things. In getting knee-deep in it, you only succeed in preempting the opportunity to enjoy life. The partner with unconditional life acceptance values the opportunity to soak up the joys of living together, while accepting the negative possibilities, without losing the forest for the trees, that is, without being obsessed with them. "These thoughts are free to come and go, and I am no worse for that!" This, again, is the *serenity* that undergirds an enduring love, the peaceful state of mind that allows two lovers to savor their time together without needless disruption. It allows them to devote themselves to one another, whether in bed, seated at the coffee table, or taking an evening stroll beneath the starry sky.

Serenity is, thus, the habitual peace of mind arising from letting go of the thorny perceptions of reality that weigh down the soul, keeping one in a state of suspended anxiety. It is a habitual mean between apathy and dogged clinging. The serene person knows the difference between the haunting thought demons and the gems of wisdom, letting the former pass freely out of mind as quickly as they arise, embracing the latter, instead. The serene person is an observer, less an evaluator. "My lover has not been honest with me," they may assert, but not, "They are no damn good." They greet reality with openness to its wonderous possibilities, but, if it happens to portend something unpleasant, they deal with the consequences without damning the universe. As such, the serene person does not needlessly disturb themselves with the vicissitudes of life.

Overcoming frustration can'tstipation through cultivating patience and perseverance

The *patient* person avoids extremes of low frustration tolerance and dogmatic perseverance. This means not giving up prematurely or needlessly going down with the ship. Patience thus entails *prudence*, that is, the capacity to perceive challenges in constructive, unproblematic ways. "Getting my MBA will take a lot of work, but it would open a lot of career opportunities for me." It then means putting in the effort. "I could feel the sweat pouring down my forehead when I studied for that exam. I wanted to throw it all away, but I hung in there and got an A." And the more you practice, the more it becomes a habit, which is precisely what patience is. It is a habit of hanging in there; of not jumping the gun; of waiting for the train to pass before trying to cross the tracks. It is a sobering virtue; the honed capacity to put off immediate gratification for long-term satisfaction.

In the bedroom, this virtue is demonstrated by not giving up if, in one moment in time, the sexual act is not brought fully to climax; for this moment is part of a stream of moments in which coming to climax is still possible. Indeed, possibilities become actualities only by allowing them to play out. "This must never happen again" blocks the momentary flow, sapping the life out of the awesome possibilities that give birth to fertile moments. Thus, enduring love is borne out of patience; for the seed to germinate, grow, and flourish. Enduring love is, thus, the succulent fruit of patience.

In the workplace, the patient manager is respected by their staff, as a result of which productivity increases. In contrast, the impatient manager produces stress, which leads to decreased productivity. Cooperation and solidarity are thus the earmarks of patience. When the patient manager comes home from work, they bring their patience with them, because virtues are not technical tools that are applied to one-quarter of life but not another. Rather, they are character traits arising from habits cultivated through practice.

Of course, a person can be more patient with one group and less with another. However, the tendency toward low frustration tolerance in one area is likely to bleed into the other. If I am an impatient partner, I am less likely to be a patient manager, and conversely. So, building the habit in one-quarter of life is likely to manifest itself in another quarter. Thus, enduring lovers, fully committed and passionately patient with one another, approach the world outside of their relationship with the zest of this secure foundation. The passion of true lovers for one another is, by no means, the same as the passion of the truly patient manager for their staff. But there is dedication in both quarters of life that gets its nourishment from the vine of patience. Suck the latter dry, and there is left the shriveled corpse of what was once a vibrant spirit infusing light into the world. Patience is the milk of enduring love.

Overcoming emotional can'*t*stipation *through cultivating temperance*

Temperance is a habit of rationally controlling your emotions. It is a mean between the extremes of overreacting and underreacting. The partner who is emotionally wired ("I've tasted tiger's blood!") is one extreme, and the partner who is "turned off" is the other ("It's all the same to me"). There is no algorithm for calculating the mean, however. It's an art, not a science. Calibrating your emotional self is a function of context. Thus, anger in one context can be temperate but not in another. If I forget your birthday, you have a right to be angry but not enraged. On the other hand, if I fail to have an erection in bed, it is temperate for you to be disappointed, but not angry. Indeed, context is king, but just how one adjusts one's emotions to the context admits of no calculus.

The emotionally *can't*stipated partner ignores context by holding onto their "can't" even when their emotional response to a situation is under- or overreactive. This is a form of emotional absolutism, a refusal, come what may, to accept your freedom, and responsibility for how you react. The consequence is forfeiture of the opportunity to resonate with your partner's emotionality. Thus, while your partner is engaged and desirous, you may be stuck on, off, or in overdrive. There is no affectionate resonance here, where two hearts meld into one, exchanging positive energies in glorious symbiosis, where each heart beats for the other. This is only possible among temperate souls who mutually adjust their emotional reactivity.

Ideally, temperate individuals do not need to control their emotions because their second nature is to respond temperately. However, this is the ideal, rarely if ever seen, this side of heaven. Even temperate people may sometimes need to reign in their emotions (or rein them out) to be in sync with their partners' emotions. So, neither you nor I are perfect; nor will we ever be. I may get worked up and regret it and so might you but it is the rebound that matters most in such cases. We realize it and get back on track, or else we go down a rabbit hole so familiar to couples whose love lives leave much to be desired.

This is not to deny that an occasional spat can add to the amorous nature of the relationship by making each partner realize how precious their love for one another truly is. This is part of being human, and the two can celebrate their mutual humanity by aspiring to love that much more in the future.

Overcoming behavioral can'tstipation *through cultivating decisiveness and courage*

Decisiveness is the habit of making and acting on one's decisions at the right time under the right circumstances. It involves realistically reposing trust in your capacity to accomplish your goals. The decisive person avoids procrastination and decisions by indecision on the one hand, and making rash decisions, on the other. The behaviorally *can't*stipated person suffers from a perceived lack of decisional capacity, whereas a decisive person takes responsibility for their capacity to make decisions as well as to act on them.

Acting is the offspring of deciding. A decision is stillborn without action. So, a decisive person is also courageous. Being courageous involves a habit of rationally controlling fear. A decisive person is courageous because they act on their best judgment and are not deterred by fear. This does not mean that courage requires fearlessness. Indeed, there are times when it is rational to fear acting, such as when doing so will cost you, your life, or your reputation. On the other hand, there are times when it is cowardly not to act, as when a loved one's well-being hangs in the balance, despite personal risk or sacrifice. Courage, hence, involves taking risks when what is at stake warrants the risk.

In intimate relationships, being decisive is part of being there for your beloved. The procrastinator generally acts too late, and the rash person too soon. So, your lover asks you to be wed and you procrastinate, not sure about whether it's the right thing to do, afraid to take the risk. They get tired of waiting and move on with their life. You fall "madly in love" (that is, have titillating sex) with someone you met last week and decide to tie the knot, only to get an annulment the next week. Both are extremes, not representative of a decisive person, or a courageous person.

In the bedroom, the decisive lover is not averse to taking risks. In contrast, the indecisive lover may stick to the same routine, unsure whether deviating from it would be a good idea. "What if I don't get it right?" Here, there is anxiety instead of excitement about the prospects of a new adventure. In contrast, the courageous lover realizes that inaction has repercussions as does action. Refusing to try new things may turn off one's lover quicker than flubbing up on something new. Still, having courage means holding off if there are overriding reasons for it. So, your friend is not sure they want to go to the next level. You are eager to move forward but you also realize that respect for personal autonomy is key to fostering intimacy, so you give your friend the space they desire.

The courage to love is essential to the cultivation of enduring love. Without the willingness to put yourself on the line, to be honest, and forthright, and to repose trust in your lover, there is no edifice upon which to anchor such a love. For to love is to act on one's vows, not just to make them. This takes decisiveness, a steadfast hand to embrace through the iffy canals of life, where outcomes are not always clear.

To decide portends the future. Decisions are always with respect to a future not yet here. Past decisions were also once future decisions, which have played out in the arena of time. So, decision-making is inherently risky because it is impossible to predict the future with certainty. These are the proverbial cards that reality has dealt us. Decisiveness to decide and courage to act are the antidotes to *can't*stipated procrastination and decision by indecision spawned by fear of the uncertain. As the chisel is to the sculptor, who carves out a likeness from stone, decisiveness, and courage are to the lover who commits to another in the medium of uncertainty and carves out a life together.

So, the question now resounds. How does a lover develop the fortitude of mind and spirit to transcend the *can't*stipating mindsets described here and acquire their counteractive virtues—self- and life-acceptance, serenity, patience, perseverance, temperance, decisiveness, and courage?

Philosophies of Self-Control

Philosophies that build self- and life-acceptance and serenity

You are not your bad thoughts

In Chapter 3, you have already had a primer on philosophical ideas that can help you to overcome self-and other-damnation and build self- and other-respect, respectively. These are the ideas of profoundly wise thinkers such as Epicurus, Aquinas, Sartre, Buddha, and Kant. Each of these philosophers would remind you that your value as a human being is not diminished or lost by having bad thoughts. As Kant admonishes, *you* are a rational, self-determining being and not a moss or a cauliflower, to use Sartre's example. Your worth and dignity, as such, are unconditionally attached to you regardless of what you imagine yourself doing. The bad thought has no power over your self-worth because the latter is non-negotiable. It is inalienable. The Buddha would admonish you that the bad thought is a transitory unreality, passing through your mind. It is a shadow, an appearance, that will sooner or later fade away; sooner if indeed you let it! Aquinas would remind you that you are infused with the Divine light, a child of God, which is for all eternity yours.

"But if I can even imagine myself doing something so horrible, doesn't that make *me* a horrible person?" Answer: Imagining yourself doing something, or feeling like doing it, is not the same as doing it. Nor is the worth and dignity of the doer the same as the bad thought. News flash: everyone has horrible thoughts! Does that make *all* of us horrible people!?

Your love for each other makes life worthwhile

As for the value of life, recall that, according to Epicurus, you have the capacity to experience very strong, pleasant feelings such as the love you feel toward your partner. This joy is what makes life worthwhile. It is, therefore, self-defeating to allow your fear of losing your partner to prevent you both from enjoying your life together. Love is the answer. Let yourself love and be loved. Give up the self-defeating obsession!

You hold the power to define your life

Existential philosophers, such as Friedrich Nietzsche and Jean-Paul Sartre, remind you that you are the author of your own life, that is, you are free to define it as you choose and are therefore responsible for it. Thus, according to Nietzsche, you are the creator of your values. "The Noble kind of man," said Nietzsche, "experiences himself as a person who determines value and does not need to have other people's approval […] He understands himself as something which in general first confers honor on things, as someone who creates values" (Nietzsche, 1954, ch. 9, sec. 260, 579). This means that life is what you proclaim it to be. So, you have no excuse if you refuse to celebrate your life and your love but, instead, choose to diminish your relationship by obsessing over bad possibilities, for this is your choice, and you are responsible for it. As Sartre (2007) would remind you, in telling yourself that you "can't" stop thinking about something bad happening to your beloved, you are acting in "bad faith," that is, lying to yourself about your freedom and responsibility in defining your life and its meanings and values (Sartre, 2007, 47–48).

So, maybe you *feel* like you can't help it, that is, you feel disempowered to stop obsessing about something bad happening. However, Sartre would admonish you that your feelings do not excuse you from your freedom and responsibility. Why? Because existentialists such as Sartre "do not believe in the power of passion. They will never regard a grand passion as a devastating torrent that inevitably compels man to perform certain acts, which, therefore, is an excuse. They think that man is responsible for his own passion" (Sartre, 2007, 29). So, like it or not, you are "condemned to be free" (Sartre, 2007, 29). The ball is, therefore, in your court!

Stop focusing on yourself

Accepting your power to let your bad thoughts go, instead of clinging to them, is key to giving up your obsessions that stand in the way of cultivating an enduring love. Paradoxically, the focus that we human beings place on *ourselves* often stands in the way of breaking this *self*-destructive habit. Did you ever think about what you really mean by your "self"? Did you ever catch it apart from the thoughts you are having? I dare say not! "I feel sad," you might say, but what you are really feeling is sadness, not yourself. "Oh, but I am the same self that I was yesterday or last year, or the year before, right?"

According to British eighteenth-century philosopher David Hume, our selves are just a bundle of perceptions (thoughts, feelings, and sensations) that are held together by memory. "As a memory alone acquaints us with the continuance and extent of this succession of perceptions, 'tis to be considered, upon that account chiefly, as the source of personal identity. Had we no memory, we never shou'd have any notion of causation, nor consequently of that chain of causes and effects, which constitute our self or person" (Hume, 2012, sec. 4).

So why even make a big deal about *yourself*? According to Buddhist monk, Thich Nhat Hanh (1998), "The idea of self is the hidden idea that there is something called "self," "me," or "mine." It's an idea that "I," "me," exist, and that there are things belonging to "me," "Me," and "mine." However, he admonishes, this idea of a self is "the center of all our grasping, of all our imagining, of all our wrong perceptions" (Hanh, 1998). But if there is no underlying self, then it is futile to make demands of yourself and then degrade yourself if these demands are not met ("*I* must not have these horrible thoughts; so, *I* am a bad person if *I* have them"). Better to simply let these "wrong perceptions" drift out of your stream of consciousness into oblivion.

Focus on your beloved's self and lose your separate selves

There is also another interesting upshot about this refocusing away from yourself. If we are all simply streams of consciousness, as the Buddhists, along with David Hume, suggest, then by focusing on other people's "selves" you can connect to their streams of consciousness and then coalesce with them.

So, in focusing on your lover's stream of consciousness, the lover and the beloved will be as one. This means listening to them, resonating with their thoughts, soaking up their consciousness, absorbing it into your own stream, and sharing your stream with them, thus allowing them to do the same. In this state of absorption, there are no separate walled-off selves, but rather one harmonious psychic unity of consciousness!

Philosophies that build patience and perseverance

Let the mud settle

In his text, *Tao Tē Ching*, ancient Chinese philosopher and founder of Taoism, Lao Tzu (1988), admonished,

> Do you have the patience to wait
> till your mud settles and the water is clear?
> Can you remain unmoving
> till the right action arises by itself?

In this profoundly important prose, Lao Tzu warns us about assuming that inaction is not itself action. How many times have you told yourself that you didn't have the patience to wait and ended up regretting it? Deliberately waiting is itself an action that, just like any other action, can have consequences. By thinking that the only recourses open to you are acts of commission, you circumscribe your options, depriving yourself of choosing to act by omission. So, doing nothing is really doing something. It has consequences. This is not to say that you should make your decisions by indecision. That's something different. What is at stake here is *choosing* not to do something as a deliberate plan of action. This is where patience comes into play, for without patience, you may, and often will, act precipitously, later regretting your choice.

So, can you remain "unmoving," sitting still until the mud settles and the water becomes clear? This does not literally mean that you remain glued to your chair or wherever you may happen to be. So, you want to move in with your partner, but they are not ready. You think it's a good idea; they don't. Do you have the patience to wait until they are ready, to let the mud settle? Or do you have low frustration tolerance, and do or say things you later come to regret? Relationships are not forged simply by positive acts (things you do); they also involve well-timed negative actions (things you don't do). Planning is a fine blend of both. Without patience, you are not likely to construct a rational plan that works.

In the bedroom, patience can make all the difference in the world. In some cases, for example, newlyweds are unable to consummate their marriage due to performance anxiety. Sometimes the two get so frustrated with each other that it only increases the anxiety and prevents consummation on further attempts. On the other hand, those who are willing to allow the mud to settle, will try again, and again, and again, until there is success! I have seen such couples end up spending the rest of their lives together, cultivating an enduring love. The same is true with the more usual cases of those who have performance anxiety and cannot have an orgasm. In such cases, patience can make the difference between a successful relationship and one that ends.

Partake in joyful perseverance

Eighth-century Indian monk, Shantideva (2005), offers this advice for persevering despite the obstacles that come with living and forging lasting relationships:

- Face frustration with "joyful perseverance," which means with enthusiasm and excitement focused on being constructive (1).
- Nothing shall "triumph" over you when you have such a positive outlook (55).
- Fulfillment comes through "strong intention, steadfastness, delight, letting go," and "readily accepting and taking control" (31–32).

There is no denying that frustration is part of life. But what would life be without it! It is simply the price you pay for being constructive. Imagine that everything was handed to you. Would it be worth as much as what you strived to build? No! This is what Shantideva means by "joyful perseverance"; it means realizing that this is what it takes to attain something of worth and value. Put in the effort and you can get what you worked for. This is exciting and you should be enthusiastic about it. With this positive attitude, you will succeed, one way or the other. If, in the end, it does not work out, then you are still a gainer for having made the journey and learned so much in the striving. Without your perseverance, however, there is no fulfillment. This takes strong intentions to succeed, steadfast devotion, delight in expending the effort toward a worthwhile goal, letting go of those thorny negative thoughts that discourage and get in the way ("I'm just a failure"; "I might as well hang it up!"). It means accepting responsibility and taking control instead of leaving your fate to chance! Sound advice for encouraging perseverance? I state my reputation on it!

Philosophies that build temperance

Your judgments about events, not the events themselves, are what upset you

One of the biggest mistakes that people make in their relationships is to suppose that their emotions are caused by things outside their control. It is, however, an ancient insight that the object of your emotion is not its cause. So, you are furious that I showed up late for our dinner date and didn't even bother to call. Didn't my failure to call *make you* furious? The answer is no. Imagine that I really did call but you missed the call—say your cell phone went automatically to voicemail. How could my not calling make you angry if I really did call? Clearly, it wasn't the (negative) event of my not calling that made you angry (because there was no such event). Rather, it was your *thought* that I didn't call that made you angry, taken together with some negative evaluation of my not having called. "They are late and didn't even have the decency to call. How could they be so inconsiderate!"

As you have seen in Chapter 1, according to the ancient stoic thinker, Epictetus (2000), what disturbs people is not the events in their lives but, rather, their judgments about these events. But these judgments are under your control. You don't have to have them. That's up to you. So, you don't have to demand I call you if I am late and think me indecent and inconsiderate if I don't. Admittedly, it would be considerate to call. But that's not the point, which is that we make ourselves upset by what we tell ourselves. Thus, you could have withheld judgment and waited for my explanation. Then you probably would not have gotten so furious. Right? Unfortunately, much of the stress we experience, daily, is needlessly generated by the failure to realize that we, ourselves, create this stress by what we tell ourselves.

Stick to judging what is in your control, not what is not

As mentioned, Epictetus (2000) also admonishes us to stick to attempting to control the things we can control, which are our own thoughts and actions, and not the things we can't control, which are the thoughts and actions of others. So, you would not try to control whether I show up late (since this is not in your control), and, therefore, would not aggravate yourself about it by making negative judgments.

Be an unattached observer of the sequences of events in the material world, not a demander

Backing up this ancient stoic wisdom is the advice of Yoga sage, Patanjali, who warned us about becoming preoccupied with causes and effects in the material world. According to this Yoga sage, these are not reality but illusions that can needlessly stir up your emotions. Instead, he recommends simply observing the sensory world without demanding anything of it. "Okay, he's late, and didn't call. I wonder what comes next." States Patanjali (2003), "when one is unattached [...] the seeds of suffering wither, and pure awareness knows it stands alone" (sutra 3.51). In other words, you will not get riled up, and, instead, see things as they truly are!

What Patanjali means by "unattached" is not clinging to things that are transitory, such as the sequences of causes and effects in the material world. These are here today and gone tomorrow, so *demanding* that they conform to some absolutistic or ideal set of rules is likely to create emotional headaches. So, it is okay to say, "I would *prefer* that my partner come on time and call when they can't" instead of "My partner *must* always be on time or call if they can't."

Philosophies that build decisiveness and courage

Have faith in yourself to succeed

Having confidence ("faith") in oneself to succeed is a condition of decisiveness, especially when the stakes are high. Pragmatist philosopher, William James (2021), makes this point quite starkly:

> [Suppose] you are climbing a mountain and have worked yourself into a position from which the only escape is by a terrible leap. Have faith that you can successfully make it, and your feet are nerved to its accomplishment. But mistrust yourself, and launching yourself in a moment of despair, you roll in the abyss (ch. 4).

How often has your loss of "faith" in your ability to handle a situation given you pause and prevented you from making a sound decision or any decision at all. In life, it is not always easy to decide and act on your decision when you believe there is much riding on it. "I need to be certain before taking that leap!" This is a recipe for decision by indecision, however, because you will never, yes never, be *certain* about life decisions. This is because all predictions about the material world are subject to error.

Faith thrives on uncertainty. If you demand certainty, there is no room for faith. It is the surrender of trust because, where there is no possibility of being mistaken, there is no meaning of trust; there is also no sense to hoping because to hope assumes that something wished for might not come to pass. Hence existentialists like Sartre have stressed the precariousness of human existence. Life is filled with probabilities, not certainties. Thus spoke Sartre (2007):

> When we want something, we always have to reckon with probabilities. I may be counting on the arrival of a friend. The friend is coming by rail or streetcar; this supposes that the train will arrive on schedule, or that the streetcar will not jump the track. I am left in the realm of possibility [...] The

moment the possibilities I am considering are not rigorously involved in my action, I ought to disengage myself from them, because no God, no scheme, can adapt the world and its possibility to my will (29).

But glorious faith, whereby you anchor trust to the realm of possibility, is what makes the devotion of lovers so precious. If all were certain, there would be nothing to risk in love. The lover who, against all odds, travels across the world to find their true love would be impossible. The fate would have already been sealed. The lover who risks everything to be with their lover would have known in advance what the outcome would be, and act accordingly. In a world of certainty, the bloom would be off the rose.

The excitement of life is, thus, rooted in possibility. In the bedroom, there is a chance that things won't go well. But when your organism is more titillating than you ever imagined, it is marvelous, not something unsurprising. For in a world of certainty, there are no surprises, not even incredibly wonderful ones!

Making mistakes is the only way you will learn

But even when you act and things do not go as planned or as you hoped they would go, you may still be the greater gainer for having tried in the first place. For it is only by trying that you will succeed; and it is only by failing, that you will learn what not to do the next time you try. This is the essence of what we mean by "scientific method," and it is the only bonified means of learning. As the esteemed British philosopher of science, Karl Popper (2001), made clear,

> To solve [...] problems, the sciences use fundamentally the same method as common sense employs, the method of *trial and error*. To be more precise, it is the method of *trying out* solutions to our problems and then discarding the false one as erroneous [...]. This procedure seems to be the only logical one (3).

So, failing at something holds the key to progress, that is, learning from your mistakes, and were there no mistakes there would be no such thing as learning. Imagine a universe in which whatever you did turned out exactly as planned each time you did it. There would be nothing to learn, no excitement of discovery; no excitement of finally succeeding after many trials. The world would be entirely as you expect, and entirely boring, devoid of the excitement of learning new things through trial and error. There is, therefore, a gift you are given each time you don't succeed, if only you recognize its sterling value going forward. Indecisiveness only breeds failure to learn. It keeps you prisoner in a stagnant universe where the prospect of success tomorrow is entombed in a cavern where fear and trepidation stand vigilant guard. Dispelling the fear of failing, sending it packing, through decisive action, is your ultimate ticket to prosperity.

See your life challenges and adversity as an opportunity to grow stronger

This is the crux of courage, for courage is no stranger to failure and adversity. The courageous person, according to existentialist Friedrich Nietzsche (1954), is elevated through their mistakes, even very big ones. Indeed, in his view, people who suffer great loss are given the opportunity to show great courage through overcoming the loss. The "discipline of suffering, of *great* suffering," admonishes Nietzsche (1954),

> [D]o you not know that only *this* discipline has created all enhancements of man so far? That tension of the soul in unhappiness which cultivates its strength, it shudders face to face with great ruin, its inventiveness and courage in enduring, preserving, interpreting, and exploiting suffering, and whatever has been granted to it of profundity, secret, mask, spirit, cunning, greatness—was it not granted to it through suffering, through the discipline of great suffering?" (p. 530)

This is not an invitation to deliberately create great hardship in your life just so that you can exercise courage. However, beware of distorting the probability of things going wrong in deciding to act, for even grand mistakes can still provide an excellent opportunity to grow wiser and stronger, and to triumph over adversity in the end. Shall you have children before you are financially secure? What if you lose your job, can't find another, and have a hungry mouth to feed? But even if you did end up down and out, the experience can be one that you carry with you throughout life, helping you to appreciate the good things. It can teach you to empathize with others who go through hard times. It can make you a much more compassionate, prudent person in the long run. And looking back, years later, when your child has grown, then ask yourself if the "suffering" was worth the price? Was that precious little girl, now a woman, worth it? Life is uncanny, and in its unpredictability, it offers great consolation that there is always the opportunity, in the struggle, to rise above misfortune, to turn it into good fortune. However, this is possible only by first taking the risk; only by having the courage to act on your decisions and then courageously confronting what comes next.

Identifying Some Core Philosophical Aspects of Self-Control

Here is a summation of some core ideas gleaned from the philosophies discussed in this chapter that can help you overcome the tendency to *can't*stipate yourself and gain the self-control essential to building an enduring, romantic love:

- Loving another person does not mean being in perfect control. Inevitably you will think or say things that do not square with the love you have for your partner. This does not mean that you are a bad person or a bad lover. It is par for the course since we are all in the same boat. We are human, after all!
- Love should not be a burden that destroys your happiness. It is, instead, a chief ingredient in making life worthwhile. Beware of squandering your love by obsessing about whether your thoughts are consistent with your love, or about the possibility of something bad happening to your loved one. Such obsessions only create anxiety that destroys the very essence of enduring, intimate love, which is to create an incredibly enjoyable life together.
- Many of us think that there are forces lying outside our control that decide our destiny. Fewer of us realize that we ourselves create this destiny by how we perceive the events in our lives. So, you might experience hard times, say financially or due to health issues, but this can be an opportunity to grow closer and stronger in love, to display great courage. You can also scuttle your relationship by fighting or blaming each other, or wallow in misfortune. This is your choice, and you have the power to choose which road to take.
- A key to choosing wisely is realizing that, while you can't control how others think, feel, and act, you can control how *you* think, feel, and act. So, it makes little sense to blame others (your partner or those outside your relationship) for how you think, feel, or act while trying to control how *others* think, feel, or act.
- Observing rather than evaluating things can promote tranquility and peace of mind (serenity). When you globally damn yourself, others, the world, or life; and when you exaggerate the risks of bad things happening or think the worst; you destroy the opportunity for interpersonal and personal happiness.
- Sometimes you may feel out of control, disempowered, like there is nothing you can do to help how you feel. But the reality is that your feelings are precisely what you *can* control. Human beings are special in this regard

because they possess the power of rational thought that can redirect or change the feelings they have. Yes, you have the power!
- All of us perceive reality through our own subjective lenses. So, it is understandable that we may become caught up in our own subjectivity and perceive this awareness as the only thing that really exists. It may feel like that there is no one else in this universe but yourself, the mysterious pilot that modulates this subjective stream of consciousness. This can present a barrier to you and your partner, who may feel the same sense of dissoluteness. But human beings have the power to transcend their individual subjective universes and share in the subjectivity of others. For example, this can happen when you empathize with what is going on in your partner's life, instead of tending to your own life.
- Human beings also have the power to refrain from acting, as well as acting. So, there are really two types of action—positive actions (commissions) and negative actions (omissions). Unfortunately, it is a common assumption that the only way to resolve problems of living, including relationship problems, is through positive action. However, sometimes the answer to a problem may lie in having patience, which means waiting, which is a negative action. Exercising the discretion to wait, rather than trying to do something else about your problems, begins with realizing that sometimes the best way to deal with the problem at hand is to be patient and wait.
- Perseverance is the child of patience. If you are patient, you will persevere in those things that you highly value. The fruit of perseverance is joyful triumph over the obstacles in life, something you are not likely to attain without the sacrifice of time and effort. Your relationship is a prime example. Working steadfastly on it, persevering, and having patience, can reap the fruits of an enduring, intimate love.
- The future is not entirely predictable, so unexpected outcomes inevitably will happen. Amidst the uncertainty of the universe, having faith that you will succeed, despite the uncertainty, can make the difference between success or fulfilling your own prophecy of failing.
- Still, fearing failure is misguided, because it is the only way we can learn how to succeed.
- A universe in which there are risks of failing is profoundly more desirable than one in which success is certain. In the latter world, life would be devoid of the excitement of triumph; for cast in stone would be the inevitable, entirely predictable, and hence boring success. In such a universe, the meaning of "success" would be empty.

Applying the Eclectic Philosophy through Cognitive–Behavioral Practice

Applying these philosophical ideas means practicing them, which involves using them to reframe your emotional, behavioral, frustrative, or cognitive "can'ts" in relating to your partner. You can work toward this goal by doing the cognitive–behavioral exercises and applying the guidelines I have provided for building self-control in your everyday life:

EXERCISE 1

Practicing Toleration

Tolerating others, such as your partner's relatives and friends, is an important part of building patience in a relationship. This exercise will help you practice building such tolerance.

1. Set up a time when you can visit someone in your partner's social or familial circle whom you find challenging to tolerate. If you do not have a tolerance issue with anyone in your partner's circle, then arrange to spend time with someone else you find difficult to tolerate. During your visit, reframe your perspective about this person, seeing them as someone who can teach you the meaning and value of tolerance.
2. Afterward, reflect on what you have learned from your experience. What, if anything, did you do right in coping with this person. What might you do differently, in the future? How does this learning experience relate to your relationship with your partner?

EXERCISE 2

Building Tolerance Through Loving Kindness Meditation

Practicing loving kindness meditation, as addressed in Chapter 2, can help you build tolerance, both inside and outside your relationship. I have already recommended that you work with the 20-minute guided "Loving Kindness Meditation" audio by Dr. Kristin Neff (n.d.) accessible online at https://self-compassion.org/guided-self-compassion-meditations-mp3-2

Practice sending out your loving kindness messages (review in Chapter 2). Include in your circle of loving kindness, those whom you have had an especially hard time getting along with, even individuals you have considered to be your enemies.

Guidelines for building self-control

- Give yourself permission to be human. Stop trying to control the thoughts that enter your mind. Just let them come and go (as you have been doing in your mindfulness training, exercise 1, chapter 1).
- Stop checking unwanted thoughts, observe but don't evaluate them, and gently push them away using your mindfulness skills. These thoughts are not the problem. Damning and catastrophizing about things—your partner, yourself, others, or the events in your life—are the problem.
- Stop trying to control what your partner thinks of you, how they feel, or what they do. Stick to what is in your power to control, namely what you think, feel, or do.
- Reframe negative situations more positively. So, things didn't go as planned in the bedroom. Try to see what you can learn from it, how you can do better next time.
- Remember, you are not perfect; neither is your partner.
- Take the focus off your own subjective world onto what's going on in your partner's subjective world. Ask them how *they* are feeling, what *they* desire, and what *they* think about things.
- Practice patience everyday: Stopped for a streetlight or caught up in rush hour traffic, don't demand that it change. When the clerk isn't helpful, don't be rude. If your lover disappoints you in bed, reassure them. Take the pressure off your relationship; let things happen at their own pace without demanding that they happen now.
- Persevere and reframe the wait as something positive, as the foreplay before the organism, as an essential part of an enduring, romantic love.
- Reframe uncertainty as that which adds excitement and vitality to life. Think about how boring life would be if everything were certain.
- Base your decisions on *probability* of outcome, not certainty. And amid the relative uncertainty of the outcome of your decision, have faith in the chance of a successful outcome rather than focusing on the possibility of failing.

In these ways, you can begin to overcome any tendency to *can't*stipate yourself emotionally, behaviorally, cognitively, and by having low frustration tolerance. This means giving up your "I can't" that stifles your relationship. This applies both inside and outside the bedroom. Love is such a delicate balance between the ways you think, feel, and act. Your willpower is like a conductor of a large symphonic orchestra that tells your thought, emotion, and behavior when to come in, how dynamic (soft or loud) to play, and when to yield to other instruments. In love, there is harmonious interplay between the dynamics of your own orchestra (thoughts, feelings, and actions) and that of your lover, where the two symphonies play as one in harmonious symbiosis. In the bedroom, you do not permit obsessive thoughts to distract your lovemaking or to alienate your lover. You abstain from acts that are unwanted or self-defeating. You do not lose patience when you both do not perform as desired. You are excited about exploring new outlets for arousal, but do not impose your will on your partner.

Inside the bedroom is a microcosm of outside it. You have patience when things do not go as planned. You view setbacks as ways to strengthen your relationship. Your affect is proportional to the situation, instead of incapacitating worry or fear. You care deeply about your partner when they suffer misfortune. So, you have the courage to make appropriate personal sacrifices in their times of need. No wonder love is such a challenging but glorious accomplishment! Of course, the musicianship is never perfect, so the goal is to continue to practice and improve the symphonic harmony. You now have at your disposal enough resources, assembled in this chapter, to build self-control in this incredibly exciting, life-long process toward an enduring, romantic love.

As you have seen, having *courage* is a vital part of this process. This means reacting proportionally to the degree of danger, putting the risks into rational perspective, without exaggerating them. In the next chapter, this aspect of building enduring, romantic love is carefully addressed.

References

Aristotle. 1941. "Nicomachean Ethics." Trans. W. D. Ross. In *The Basic Works of Aristotle*, ed. by Richard McKeon, 930–1112. New York: Random House.

Cohen, Elliot D. 2022. *Cognitive Behavior Therapy for Those Who Say They Can't: A Workbook for Overcoming Your Self-Defeating Thoughts*. New York: Routledge.

Damasio, Antonio R. 1994. *Descartes' Error: Emotion, Reason, and The Human Brain*. New York: Putnam.

Epictetus. 2000. *Enchiridion*, Trans. E. Carter. The Internet Classic Archive. http://classics.mit.edu/Epictetus/epicench.html.

Hanh, Thich Nhat. 1998. "Sutra on The Middle Way. Dharma Talk in Plum Village, France." A Buddhist Library. http://www.abuddhistlibrary.com/Buddhism/G%20-%20TNH/TNH/The%20Sutra%20on%20the%20Middle%20Way/I/Dharma%20Talk%20given%20by%20Thich%20Nhat%20Hanh%20on%20March%2015.htm.

Hume, David. 2012. *A Treatise of Human Nature*. Project Gutenberg. https://www.gutenberg.org/files/4705/4705-h/4705-h.htm.

James, William. 2021. *The Will to Believe and Other Essays in Popular Philosophy*. Project Gutenberg. https://www.gutenberg.org/cache/epub/26659/pg26659-images.html.

Lao-Tzu. 1988. *Tao Te Ching*, Trans. Stephen Mitchell. https://www.organism.earth/library/document/tao-te-ching.

Nietzsche, Friedrich. 1954. "Beyond Good and Evil." Trans. H. Zimmern. In *The Philosophy of Nietzsche*, 369–616. New York: Random House.

Patanjali. 2003. *The Yoga-Sutra of Pantanjali: Sanskrit-English Translation & Glossary*, Trans. Chip Hartranft. Internet Archive. https://archive.org/details/chip-hartranft-sanskrit-english-translation-glossary-the-yoga-sutra-of-patanjali.

Popper, Karl. 2001. *All Life is Problem Solving*. New York: Routledge.

Sartre, Jean-Paul. 2007. *Existentialism is a Humanism*, Trans. Carol Macomber. New Haven: Yale University Press (Kindle ed.). https://www.amazon.com/Existentialism-Humanism-Jean-Paul-Sartre/dp/0300115466?asin=0300115466&revisionId=&format=4&depth=1.

Shantideva. 2005. *Engaging in Bodhisattva Behavior*, Trans. A. Berzin, Study Buddha, Berzin Archives. https://studybuddhism.com/en/tibetan-buddhism/original-texts/sutra-texts/engaging-in-bodhisattva-behavior/perseverance.

CHAPTER 5

BUILDING COURAGE IN ROMANTIC LOVE

> Who could refrain that had a heart to love and in that heart courage to make love known?
>
> —William Shakespeare, *Macbeth*.

Recognizing Catastrophizing as an Impediment

Do you spend a lot of time in your relationship talking about problems rather than enjoying the moment? Does one problem seem to replace the other in an endless procession with a few glimpses of light interspersed between problems that seem insurmountable or of such a magnitude of importance as to require your immediate attention? Do you look to your partner to help you resolve these problems so that even the prospect of spending an intimate time together plays second (or third) fiddle to these perceived problems?

You are not the only one who lives like this, for there are countless couples who squander their lives, their relationships, and their happiness by submerging themselves in the perceived problems of everyday life. Perhaps, your partner has appealed to your reason, asking for a reprieve in this ongoing ritual of cleansing yourself of the problems that so occupy your psyche. Perhaps, you have not, infrequently, dismissed these pleas for mercy as irresponsible, since the problem must take precedence over forging an intimate relationship, which can always wait until tomorrow. But tomorrow never seems to come, for there is always the almighty problem that looms in the background, chilling off the prospects for intimacy.

In the bedroom, sex feels like a diversion from the problems of living, a sort of oasis in a desert, rather than a seamless and complimentary part of your relationship, like a medication you have taken to anesthetize the pain, only to soon wear off. And, even during the sexual act, or foreplay, the problems just seem to have retreated, not truly gone away. There is, hence, anxiety playing in the background that distracts you from experiencing the melding of souls that is emblematic of love, as distinct from *just* having sex. So, you can manage to just have sex, even orgasmic sex, although not very special sex.

The description I have painted above may match you to one degree or another. If it, indeed, seems a lot like you, then you tend to *catastrophize* about the perceived problems of living. This means that you exaggerate just how bad things are.

There are two types of catastrophizing. In one version, the *future-oriented* type, it is coupled with the magnification of risks. So, first, you exaggerate the probabilities of something bad happening. Then you say how horrible, terrible, and awful it would be. "If I don't get to bed on time, then I will not be able to concentrate on my exam, I will fail it, and I will never get my degree! That would be horrible, the worst thing that could happen to me. I'll be a total flop!" This thinking creates intense anxiety. The executive part of your brain (the part that does practical thinking and decision-making) signals your amygdala (the part of your brain that prepares you for fight or flight). In this state, your adrenals pump adrenaline into your bloodstream, which increases your heart rate, which makes it hard to fall asleep. As a result, you may, indeed, do poorly on the exam by keeping yourself up all night and stressing yourself out!

The other type of catastrophizing is *then-and-now-oriented*. This arises when something undesirable *has happened* or is *presently happening* and you tell yourself how awful, horrible, or terrible it is that it happened or is happening. This type of catastrophizing tends to produce a depressed mood or feelings of hopelessness. "I didn't get the job that I wanted. Now my life is over!" "I just found out that I have diabetes. I might as well end it all now!"

If you tend to find reasons not to do things because you think they carry too much risk, then you probably engage in future-oriented catastrophizing. As a result, you may condemn yourself and your partner to a humdrum existence. In the extreme, this may involve phobic thinking such as in the case of agoraphobia where one is afraid to venture outside the house. If this is you, then you may need to undergo systematic exposure (slowly coming out of your shell) under the direction of a therapist (American Psychological Association, n.d.).

If you tend to be risk-aversive in bed, then you probably bore your sex partner by dismissing any suggestions about experimenting with different sexual activities. Instead, you may insist on traditional intercourse and refuse to have oral–genital or other alternative types of sex. Anal sex is out of the question because it's "dirty" and can cause anal ruptures. "Who would want to have something pushed up your rectum anyway!" Moreover, should you reluctantly agree to try something new, and "less safe," you may experience intense anxiety about it that destroys the prospect for success. You expect things to go wrong even before they do go wrong, and, as a result, they do!

Likewise, outside the bedroom, people who engage in future-oriented catastrophizing tend to stick to the same social activities. They may insist on going to the same ("tried and true") restaurants or other social outlets, thereby forcing their partners to lead a very predictable, although boring existence.

You may also view life from a jaundice perspective. Invariably, bad things do happen. As a result, you become preoccupied with these things, which negatively colors your perception of the here and now, and of your prospects. Feeding this sullen attitude is a tendency to oversimplify reality through overgeneralizing. That is, because something bad has happened, you infer that it's *all* bad and that the *entire* universe sucks.

Relationships suffer immensely, as a result. One client, whose partner was a then-and-now-oriented as well as a future-oriented catastrophizer, once described his situation as "going into a dark tunnel and occasionally coming out into the light only to go back into the tunnel." The garden stock of every day, negative events took on an air of gloom and doom for his partner. A child getting picked on by the school bully became a crisis to be ruminated about *ad nauseam*. "How can you be so calm when this is happening to our child!" Not surprisingly, when the bully was disciplined by the teacher and backed off, another crisis emerged behind it—this time bad grades! So, the child finally got some help and scored an A, and all was well—but only for a brief time until a new crisis was perceived. This time, the air conditioner broke down on a hot, summer day, just one day after the machine went out of warranty. "Horror of horrors, it never ends!" Indeed, there *is* no hope in sight for those who chronically catastrophize, for, if you are on the lookout, you shall likely find something to turn into a catastrophe.

No doubt, you are also familiar with expressions such as "Caught between a rock and a hard place" and "Damned if you do, and damned if you don't." These nicely sum up the tendency of those who catastrophize to paint dilemmas and then stew in them. "No matter what we do, we're screwed. Here's what one client told his partner during the COVID pandemic: "If we stay in the house and don't go near other people, we'll be miserable and go crazy; and if we go near other people, we'll each probably get COVID and end up dying in a hospital COVID ward, all alone, without each other. No matter what we do it's so horrible!"

This couple ended up staying in their house for two years with virtually no exposure to the outside world. They would order their groceries through Instacart and would spend hours washing them off in their garage before they even brought them into their house. Sadly, it was not the virus that destroyed the quality of life this couple led for two entire years. Rather, what had this regrettable result was the tendency to oversimplify reality by thinking in black or white terms ("Either we live in total isolation from others, or we go out and expose ourselves to the virus") and then catastrophize about each of these mutually exclusive alternatives. Veritably, there were other alternatives, such as exercising caution in socializing; for example, social distancing and wearing masks.

Building Courage in Romantic Love

In this video, I discuss catastrophizing as an impediment to making love and the importance of exercising courage inside (and outside) the bedroom.

https://youtu.be/EVmRtbgFT4I

Identifying Virtues that Counter Catastrophizing: Courage, Foresightedness, and Objectivity

Courage

In speaking about courage, you may have an image of a person who runs into a burning building to save a child. Indeed, such are the tales of heroes. But courage is not the same as heroism. While heroes are courageous, not all courageous people are heroes. Courage, said Aristotle (1941), is the mean between the two extremes of rashness and cowardice. To act rashly, means you are not afraid enough; and to act in a cowardly manner, means you are too afraid. Courage is thus *rational* fear control. You are courageous when you are in the habit of exercising your rational judgment in taking risks. Taking bold risks does not make you courageous if these risks are not reasonable ones—where there is a reasonable chance of attaining something of value that is worth the risk.

Courage is exercised not only in crises, such as on the battlefield but also in everyday life because, in life, there are often situations that call for the exercise of judgment and carry risk. Being too afraid to make a commitment to someone you love is cowardly; proposing marriage to your date whom you have known for one night because you enjoyed the sex, is to be rash, not courageous. There is no such thing as being "too courageous" or "not courageous enough" because being courageous means that you are neither too afraid nor not afraid enough. As Aristotle admonishes (1941), determinations of right or wrong depend on the situation. In some situations, taking big risks is rational (when the goal is noble and achievable); in other situations, taking such risks may be rash (when the goal is not noble, or it is not achievable).

Couples who are in love are prepared to take substantial risks for each other. Would you be willing to take a bullet for your beloved? In enduring love, this rings true. But it is not enough to be willing to take a bullet for your beloved to be courageous in love. For courage is demonstrated in your willingness to make commitments to your loved one, to be there for this person on a regular basis, even if this involves personal sacrifice; to not abandon your beloved in hard times.

Once there was a young man of 17 years who met his future wife, then just 16, just before he went off to college out of state, far away. This was during the Vietnam War and the young man had a college deferment. However, after two months away from his girlfriend, his burning desire to be with her continued to grow and he was unable to concentrate on his studies. The young man decided to drop out of college to be with his girlfriend. Immediately, the draft board reclassified him. A draft lottery occurred, and the young man scored low, a 31, which meant that he was to be inducted into the armed forces. Very risky, indeed! Was the young man's act of leaving college to be with his girlfriend rash or was it courageous?

Sometimes, the answer is controversial. I often think about this because this young man was me. After 50 years, I am still married to the same woman; and I do not know if that would have been true today had I remained in college. But I can say this, that I love this ever so beautiful woman with all my heart and soul; and I do not have any regrets.

Having had this hiatus in my formal education gave me a stronger appreciation for the value of a college education, so, when I finally had the opportunity to return to college (my wife and I went to the same college and we were wed when we were sophomores), I devoted myself to my studies with immense passion.

Possessing the virtuous habit of courage does not mean that you will always do the courageous thing, since you are, after all, human. But it does mean that you will *tend* to act courageously. Whether or not my act was courageous, it emanated from the stuff of courage, that of proportioning the risks taken to the value of what was at stake. I valued being with my future wife more than anything, or almost anything, else, so I was willing to take the risk.

Foresightedness

Hindsight, it is commonly said, is better than foresight. How often have we regretted our decisions when they have turned out badly. So, you look back and think, if only I had done things differently. But here is the rub. You really don't know how the future would have unfolded had you done things differently. For changing one link in a causal chain of events changes everything else, and what emerges miles down that causal chain is not knowable. So, you go for a Sunday drive and get into a fender bender. "If I stayed home this wouldn't have happened!" True, but you do not know what else could have happened had you stayed home, and what would have subsequently happened, as a result. Instead of taking your car to the repair shop, on Monday, you would be doing something else, which opens a whole new line of future unknown possibilities. So, hindsight is also not what it is cracked up to be, for your knowledge of the future is always uncertain.

Still, in navigating the future, there are rational approaches and ones that are not rational. One irrational approach is to demand certainty when there is no such thing. Another irrational approach is the other extreme of supposing that, because the future is uncertain, it does not matter what you do, the view that "All of life is just a crapshoot." The mean between these extremes is what I mean by foresight. This mean consists of basing your judgments about the future on the *probability* or outcomes. So, if you enroll in a computer science program, there is no guarantee that you will get a job, but, if you did your homework and discovered that there is a growing demand for this area, then you are exercising foresight. This is the ability to generalize about the material world and make predictions about the future that are probable relative to the facts, as known. A person who possesses foresight tends to use past experience successfully in making life decisions.

Such a person can cope effectively in the material universe, where there are only degrees of probability, not certainty.

It is also important to distinguish between being *justified* and being correct. So, you go into computers after researching the job market, but other people are thinking like you, the supply of job applicants exceeds the demand, and you are still unable to get a job when you graduate. Here, chastising yourself, for being wrong, is not very helpful, for you were *justified* in your decision, even though it did not turn out as you expected. In this world of uncertainty, being justified is what you want to be, for it is more likely to get you where you want to go than deciding on a whim.

Having hindsight is also a counteractive to future-oriented catastrophizing. In the latter, as you have seen, you magnify the risks of bad things happening and then say how awful these things are. "If I can't even get a job now that I have my degree, I will never get one!" Perhaps, however, there is an area of specialization, a certificate program, that can fine-tune your credentials and land you a job. Foresight is not perfect, but it is still your best asset in navigating your ship of life.

Sadly, I have seen many couples drift apart because of everyday life struggles, such as lack of job security, where a major problem lies in their ability to navigate the future with foresight. Enduring love does not just happen. It is a product of rational living, which means knowing how to navigate the headwaters of the future by cultivating a habit of rational decision-making. Foresightedness is at the helm of this vessel, without which, you are like a seaman adrift at sea, without a compass and no direction home, searching aimlessly for the shore.

The anxiety generated by future-oriented catastrophizing, due largely to a lack of foresight in assessing risks, can seep into every aspect of your relationship. In the bedroom, you fear the worst that could happen. "What if I don't give my partner an orgasm? That would mean they don't really love me. What a loser that would make me. How horrible!" In the throes of anxiety, you bring about just what you fear. You are stilted, unsure, thinking about what your partner might be thinking of you, and not really present in the act itself. So, your erection falls short; and you think the worst of yourself, and your lover.

On a romantic rendezvous with your mate, a candle-lit dinner at an exquisite Italian restaurant, a palmetto bug scurrying across the clean white tablecloth, no compliments of the world-renowned chef, can sully your appetite and destroy the potential for a remarkable prelude to lovemaking. "How dreadful!" you say! Your magnification of this small insect, so miniscule in its significance, gone in an instant, now steals the show; sexual intimacy falls flat, and the evening ends with a bug-eyed memory, instead of a romantic interlude.

For those who catastrophize, when small things go wrong, they take on an aura of great big things because they become the grounds for predicting further, future outcomes. The bug becomes an ominous sign of more of the same to come. There is no rebounding from an unpleasant instant because it means that the rest of the night is mysteriously tainted by the gigantic shadow cast by a small bug. Reigning in this tendency is of the greatest importance in forging an enduring, romantic love. This means cultivating foresightedness; and being careful not to exaggerate the implications of the relatively insignificant everyday happenstance. The probability of a bug polluting an opportunity for romance is only as great as you decide it to be. Being foresighted, here, means that you put the proverbial bug (whatever the small happenstance may be) into perspective and see it for what it is. The probabilities change only when *you* change them by magnifying risks based on fear, not evidence. Fear is, thus, no substitute for evidence, unless you make it so.

Some couples love each other so much that they fear something happening to them. So, your loved one has not come home, as expected, and they do not answer their phone. Have they gotten into an accident? Are they lying in an alley somewhere beaten to death? Have they had a heart attack? These demons may invade your thoughts and leave you feeling a deep sense of fear, as thought these things have already happened. The imagination can feel quite real because it uses the same parts of the brain that are used in the thoughts of real events (University of Colorado at Boulder, 2018). But don't be taken in by the fact that the object of this fear feels real; it is just fear. There is no evidence that these things are real. Foresightedness involves basing your judgments on evidence, not fear.

Objectivity

The objective lover sees reality in all its diversity and nuance and not in terms of two damning alternatives. Nor do they view reality in terms of all or nothing, always or never. For reality rarely conforms to such absolutes. There is disappointment in love as well as titillating climaxing. There is poor judgment sometimes exercised; sometimes there is blatant disregard. But there are also regrets and apologies; kissing and making up after a quarrel; peaceful nights and ones that are tumultuous.

Love is not a contest to win or lose. A lover is not the bounty that one claims triumphantly. Lovers do not themselves compete with one another for leadership. For, in a loving relationship, there is a division of labor, autonomously established, but not a leader and follower, or ruler and subject, because enduring lovers eschew such bifurcations, and embrace equal partnership.

Nevertheless, it is often assumed that, in a functional relationship, there must always be a head of household and a subordinate to carry out the commands of the former. The domineering party takes the reigns while the other party passively follows. After all, someone must be the leader, right? Wrong! Love is unity, not division. "Leader" and "follower" represent the language of division. "Partnership" represents the language of unity, for in a true partnership, there is mutuality and respect for each partner as an equal. It is by oversimplifying human reality, by turning all the forces of socialization to infuse acceptance of such an ideology of oppression, that it has been able to operate, silently, in human relationships, stifling the freedom that is essential to enduring love. Oppressed followers do not make creative and fulfilling life partners; nor do they make romantic lovers. Meeting each other, whether inside or outside the bedroom, as equals, releases the sexual and life energies of each partner to comingle and coalesce as one. This manifests itself in the magical feeling of love that cannot be mistaken for the counterfeit relationship that grows out of the bondage of an unequal relationship.

Traditionally, it was the man who was expected to be the master, whereas the woman was expected to be his handmaiden, or servant. But, while this is one manifestation of an unequal heterosexual relationship, this is by no means the only one. Women have sometimes assumed the leadership role and subordinated their male counterparts, and in homosexual relationships, one party to the relationship has subordinated the other too. In none of these relationships is there likely to be enduring love, however.

Eventually, such unequal relationships become boring, meaningless, and lacking in vitality. Ask a woman, who has been an obedient servant for most of her adult life, to a man who has sucked her dry. She will carry herself, with pride, for her devotion to her husband, and to her children, whom she has raised. But ask her if she is truly happy, and would not have traded this for an enduring, romantic love, where she was an equal partner in the relationship. She may well fall back on the tradition into which she has been socialized, announcing that this is what a woman is supposed to do with her life. But there will always be a somber hint of discontent in the voices of such women, who may never admit that they have not attained the kind of love that transcends the humdrum traditions into which they have been indoctrinated.

She will not breathe a word of her true sentiments to her spouse about the regrets that privately go on in her mind when she reflects on what might have been had she been a full partner, in her own right, and not a possession of another. As for her spouse, ask him if he too silently wishes to have had an autonomous, free, and vital partner, rather than a possession. If he can bracket his rationalizations for a moment and wonder what it might have been like to have been free of the stress of having to live up to her expectations of his always being a masterful leader, what might his private thoughts be? Veritably, true love defies relationships based on false bifurcations such as master and servant.

This also applies to bifurcations of character. The beloved is neither a saint nor a devil, even during laudable acts of heroism or condemnable acts of betrayal, because human reality is not so simplistically pigeon-holed, with most human behavior falling somewhere in between. Objective lovers realize that their lovers, as human beings, can do both good and bad, and, therefore, do not engage in such oversimplifications of human reality.

Objective lovers are also optimistic but are not bedazzled by bearers of false gifts. They are not naïve and easily taken in by phonies and charlatans, who seductively feign love, for ulterior motives, out of sociopathy, narcissism, or a false sense of entitlement. The objective lover sees through such schemes.

Objective lovers also see gender stereotypes ("bitch," "ditz," "flaming," "macho," "henpecked," and the rest of this sorry lot) for what they are distortions of human reality. People are complicated creatures. True lovers do not love stereotypes of persons; they love persons. Those who do not know how to love others (or themselves) attempt to classify people according to such fixed, rigid oversimplifications. As a result, they never get to know people for who they truly are, and thus never give themselves an opportunity to love *them*.

Philosophies that Build the Virtues that Counter Catastrophizing

Philosophies that build courage

Courage is the mean between too much and too little fear

It is often thought that to be courageous you must be willing to do something ultra-risky, like running into a burning building to save someone. Indeed, whether in real life or in the fictional depictions of true love in the movies, enduring lovers have been willing to lay down their lives to save their loved ones. But you don't have to sacrifice your life for your lover to exhibit courage, for courage is demonstrated in what you do during everyday life. As you have seen in Chapter 4, according to Aristotle (1941), courage is a *mean* between the extremes of too little fear (rashness) and too much fear (cowardice). Hence, any time in life's daily activities, when you rationally control your fear, you are being courageous. Are you afraid to stick to your moral principles because there is a risk that you will suffer a loss, for example, lose your job or the friendship of another? Sometimes it's worth standing on principle and it is, therefore, *morally* courageous to do so. Are you afraid to tell your partner what they need to hear for fear that they will get angry at you? Sometimes this is the courageous thing to do because your partner will suffer a much greater slight for not hearing what you have to say.

So, it is very much about context or situation. Sometimes it's just not worth the sacrifice ("If I tell them what I really think, they will withhold the funding and we'll be even worse off"). It may not be the right time or place ("My partner is not emotionally prepared just yet for this bad news"); or there may be another principle that may be overriding ("Honesty may not be the best policy when human lives hang in the balance!"). So exercising courage means controlling how afraid you are, according to what is reasonable *under the given circumstances*. Here, the standard of whether the amount of fear you have is reasonable consists of a mean (point of moderation) between too much fear and too little.

Are you a courageous lover according to this view? Paradoxically, the courageous lover may be more fearful than a cowardly person in some situations. For example, if you truly love your partner then you may greatly fear insulting them. "Nor is a man a coward if he fears insult to his wife […]," says Aristotle (1941, bk. 3, ch. 6). For strong fear may not be excessive in such a situation. But do you fear criticism from you partner? If you are afraid to accept constructive, well-intended criticism and you become self-defensive in the face of it, then this fear may be cowardly. This would apply, too, in very sensitive situations, such as in the bedroom. Thus, it can be courageous to listen attentively and compassionately to your partner about how you could better please them, and to try your best to better satisfy them during your next sexual encounter.

Knowledge is an antidote to fear

In his essay entitled, "Courage," American philosopher, Ralph Waldo Emerson (1904), states:

> Knowledge is the antidote to fear—Knowledge, Use and Reason, with its higher aids. The child is as much in danger from a staircase, or the fire-grate, or a bath-tub, or a cat, as the soldier from a cannon or an ambush. Each surmounts the fear as fast as he precisely understands the peril and learns

the means of resistance. Each is liable to panic, which is, exactly, the terror of ignorance surrendered to the imagination. Knowledge is the encourager, knowledge that takes fear out of the heart, knowledge and use, which is knowledge in practice (p. 263).

Emerson is telling you that knowledge can make you courageous if you are prepared to use it to make rational judgments about danger. Ignorance and an active imagination can catapult a small risk into a giant one, unless it is tempered by knowledge. The skilled surgeon has less to fear, even if the surgery being performed is complex. This is not to say that knowledge does not expose danger and give reason to be afraid. The child who burns his hand on the hot stove displays little fear and learns by experience. The knowledge thus gained provides a basis for safely navigating the danger in the future.

The danger of a relationship failing follows suit, and there is, often, less to fear when you draw on the knowledge you gain from listening to what your partner has to say about their world. Quite often, relationships suffer because partners do not listen and learn. "I hate it when you squeeze me like that" becomes a beacon of light guiding you toward improving your sex life. Indeed, relationships grow increasingly stronger with the expanse of knowledge acquired over a lifetime.

An almost imperceptible look one partner gives another can communicate volumes for partners whose knowledge of each other is finely calibrated due to years of listening and learning about each other. On the other hand, some partners do not seem to have a clue as to what the other is thinking or feeling. The former relationship has the propensity to support an enduring love; the latter does not and has a much greater likelihood of failing. So, love and knowledge, especially knowledge of each other's subjective world (thoughts, feelings, desires, values, etc.), are interdependent. If you love your partner, you will be inclined to learn more about her, and if you have more knowledge of her, you will be more likely to cultivate a loving relationship. Of course, this does not mean that such knowledge can't expose negative aspects of your partner that dampen the relationship. It is rather that a relationship without such reciprocal knowledge is likely not to flourish, or to fail.

Accordingly, courageous lovers seek reciprocal knowledge, and keep learning more and more about each other over a lifetime. As this knowledge base grows, so does the relationship flourish, and the fear of it failing diminishes. Imperiled relationships are just the opposite. Ignorance breeds fear and mistrust, which can lead eventually to the dissolution of the relationship. Thus, the courage to love entails the courage to learn as much as you can about your lover, both positive as well as negative traits. For navigating a relationship, like all other things in this imperfect world, involves knowing your way around the entire range of attributes. A courageous sailor in love with the sea knows what to do in times of great turbulence, and the sea is then just as majestic and beautiful to them, even when, and perhaps even more so, when it is most dangerous; for they know their way around this danger. For the courageous lover, the fire in their beloved's deep green eyes, ignited by a quarrel, invites a gentle caress, a word of solace, an apology, an empathic appreciation, that extinguishes the flames of disengagement or falling apart. It is but foreplay to reaffirmation of committed love, sealed with a kiss, erecting a milestone on the road to enduring, romantic love.

The sudden changes and accidents of life invite cheerful courage

As discussed in Chapter 1, the ancient Stoics remind us that the things in our control are our own thoughts, feelings, and actions, while the things not in our control are the thoughts, feelings, and actions of others, as well as whatever else transpires in the world not arising from our own actions. According to these philosophers, courage thus lies in not catastrophizing over those things in the latter category, but rather, as Roman Stoic, Marcus Aurelius (2001), holds, "in all things to endeavour to have power of myself, and in nothing to be carried about; to be cheerful and courageous in all sudden chances and accidents, as in sicknesses [...]" (loc. 344–346). So, courage lies in being "cheerful" even about the "sudden chances and accidents" of life that are not of your own doing. For, since you have no power over these things but only over yourself, there is no point to disturbing yourself about them. Such courage, manifested in calmness of mind in confronting such happenstances, instead of the panic and calamity of framing a catastrophe, increases your potential for attaining an enduring love.

This does not mean that you should insulate yourself from being there, emotionally, in undesirable circumstances. Quite the contrary, it is in your power to console your loved one when they suffer, or to show empathy for them, or for others, when they are suffering. You can also do what you can to address misfortunes, for example, enlisting quality medical care in the case of sickness. These are positive contributions you can make in addressing such unfortunate events, without losing your calmness of mind. In fact, you are less likely to be of service to your loved one if you panic and thereby lose your ability to cope. Courage, as said, avoids the extremes—both over- and underreacting to perceived danger. For the Stoic thinkers, losing your cool over things outside your control is to overreact, because it is self-defeating: you spin your wheels and get nowhere except to upset yourself unnecessarily. Of course, as humans we sometimes overact; but this is not the same as habitually doing so. The courageous person, on the Stoic account, is in a *habit* of not overacting to things beyond one's control. But this does not mean you must be perfect.

Being strong for your lover, not being distracted by fear of factors outside your control, can allow you to be present with your lover, to support them, and take care of them when they need you the most. This can strengthen your love. The hard times you have gone through together, successfully getting through them, can bring you closer together; and as I have repeatedly emphasized, an essential aspect of enduring love is unity.

The sexual aspect of enduring love is the same. Being able to love passionately, especially during difficult times, without being distracted by things outside your control, can help you both get through those times, and emerge from them, stronger than ever. Obsessing over danger, catastrophizing about it, only adds to the suffering, and places a damp blanket over the bedroom sheets. "We will first have to get through this crisis before we can make love" thwarts progress toward enduring, romantic love. If you get on this bandwagon, your lovemaking will be regularly interrupted by the vicissitudes of life that crop up in endless procession over a lifetime. So, instead of strengthening your relationship through romantic lovemaking, you stifle your relationship by putting your love life on hold. Courageous lovers are not afraid to make love during difficult times. To the contrary, they inspire it.

Philosophies that build foresightedness

Risks are inevitable no matter what you do, or don't do

How many times have you felt sure that something would happen, and it didn't? Therein lies the plight of humanity. We naturally plan for the future, but at the same time cannot be certain what that future will be. The gap between the now-and-then and the future is impassable because, as time passes, the future becomes the now-and-then and is replaced by the future. So, waiting for the future to reveal itself before acting to change it is in vain.

Sadly, potentially great love may never materialize because of the fear of taking risks. However, you have no choice but to take risks, like it or not, because *not* doing something also plays out in the future. So, you decide not to marry your sweetheart and end up without a true love until your dying day. You look them up online and find that they are married with two children, and you are alone. "Had I not been afraid to make the commitment, this could have been me!" Of course, you do not know if this could have been you had you been wed.

But there is no love without commitment; no children without conception; no marriage without be wedding.

As Sartre (2007) starkly asserted, "Man is nothing other than his own project. He exists only to the extent that he realizes himself, therefore he is nothing more than the sum of his actions, nothing more than his life" (p. 37). It is not sufficient to imagine the future without acting on it, for "dreams, expectations, and hopes," says Sartre, "only serve to define a man as a broken dream, aborted hopes, and futile expectations; in other words, they define him negatively, not positively" (p. 38). So, the future makes no promises; yet without making plans and acting on them, you relinquish the possibility of actualizing your dreams, hopes, and expectations, and thus *define yourself* negatively in terms of such missed possibilities.

Past experience affords us degrees of probability, never certainty

The practical implication of the above is clear. The future may not be certain, but there are possibilities that can become actualities through one's actions. Further, these possibilities can be assessed in terms of their strength, through rational thinking. As the British contemporary philosopher, Bertrand Russell (2013), made plain, there are degrees of probability that you can assess, based on your past experience:

> The fact that two things have been found often together and never apart does not, by itself, suffice to prove demonstratively that they will be found together in the next case we examine. *The most we can hope is that the oftener things are found together, the more probable it becomes that they will be found together another time* [...] (p. 65, my italics)

Clearly, you can learn from experience and profit from it in the future if you are open to evidence of the past in making your decisions about the future. I have known aspiring lovers who have kept relating the same way over, and over again for a lifetime to no avail. One couple was married for 60 years and almost every day of that expansive chunk of time was spent bickering with each other. Generally, after an argument, there were moments of peace and expressed determination, on each of their parts, to be more open to one another's differences. But, shortly after these vows were taken, the couple was back at it again.

Predictably, unless a new, different approach was adopted, there would be no likely departure from the past, which would continue to be repeated *ad nauseam*. This senseless pattern was partly due to the inertia of having lived like this for so many years, and partly due to the absolutistic idea that each partner had to live up to an image of what each thought was true, right, or good. So, when one partner seemed to fall short of this image, the other would persist trying to set reality straight. Sadly, each partner wanted the other to fit such a perfectionistic idea because each cared deeply about the other. But this devotion was wasted on constant bickering. Taking Russell's advice of proportioning their beliefs about the future to the past would have helped the couple to give up the old dysfunctional way of relating and trying something different, such as going to couples counseling to help them overcome their inertia.

If people resemble each other in one or more respects, be careful about jumping to conclusions that they resemble each other in other respects

"You are just like [...]." Filling in the dots with someone you dislike, have you ever launched this torpedo at your partner? It is a popular mode of attack. First you claim that your partner has something in common with another person, who also has some further undesirable feature, and then you predict that your partner will prove to be like this other person in this other respect too. "My friend's spouse cheated on them, and they travel a lot just like you, so you're probably cheating on me too. How could I ever trust you again!" So, you put your spouse on trial and find them guilty. Unfortunately, this is a miscarriage of justice; for the evidence upon which you convicted your spouse is insufficient, and a person is innocent until proven guilty in our system of justice.

The evidence is insufficient because you did not consider relevant differences between your friend's spouse and your own. For example, you have been married to yours for five years and, to your knowledge, they have never cheated on you; however, your friend's spouse has a history of cheating, even before they were married. So, be careful to look at not just the similarities but also the *differences* before you use comparisons as a basis to draw inferences.

As philosopher and logician, John Stuart Mill (1882), makes clear, there are two considerations to consider in making such inferences:

1. Two things resemble each other in one or more respects; a certain proposition is true of the one; therefore, it is true of the other [...].
2. [I]t is clear [however], that *every dissimilarity which can be proved between them furnishes a counter-probability of the same nature on the other side* (pp. 394–395).

So, the fact that your partner bears some resemblance to someone who cheats, does not mean that they also cheat, because there may also be a dissimilarity that yields "a counter-probability on the other side." Thus, if you just consider (1) and fail to consider (2), you can make a grandiose error: convicting your partner of a misdeed for which they may not be guilty.

Again, it's about probability, not certainty. Will you ever be able to predict with certainty that your partner is not cheating? No, because in the material world, nothing is 100% certain. But, in true love, there is commitment and trust that transcends the need for certainty. Indeed, the concept of trust would make no sense in a world where the devotion of one's partner was guaranteed!

This trust is not blind, however. It does not shrink from the evidence. Some relationships are disqualified as trustworthy by disconfirming evidence. On the other hand, true lovers do not fabricate or perceive misdeeds in the absence of evidence and are open to the possibility that they have misunderstood the facts. As love grows, so does trust, and the evidence of everyday encounters with the beloved supports it, even though it can never prove with absolute certainty that one's beloved is faithful. There is, thus, a rational theology in true love, a faith in the beloved, that grows steadfastly over time and experience, as the relationship ripens, but which never reaches absolute certainty. It is this faith-based aspect of enduring, romantic love that contributes to its transcendent, sacrosanct quality.

Philosophies that build objectivity

In love there is a Yin in every Yang

In his famous book, *Tao Te Ching*, Chinese philosopher, Lao Tzu (2017), the founder of Daoism, famously states,

All things carry Yin
yet embrace Yang.
They blend their life breaths
in order to produce harmony (ch. 42).

Yin is associated with the negative, such as darkness, and Yang with the positive, such as light. But all things include both.

Life is a harmonious balance of both. In love, there are feelings of joy and sadness. When lovers quarrel, there is also resolution and harmonious relationships amid individual differences. Indeed, without a Yin there cannot be a Yang, and conversely, so that neither is more or less important nor real. "My way or the highway" displays a lack of harmony between Yin and Yang because it attempts to drive a wedge between these two essential aspects of reality that cannot exist separately. Living happily means living in harmony with Yin–Yang, not in terms of false bifurcations of reality.

In the bedroom, sexual tension is relieved through orgasm, and there is fusion and unity of two bodies melded into harmonious unison in the very act. "Satisfy me!" is the language of exclusion, a craving for the Yang without the Yin, whereas "My orgasm is not without yours" is the fusion of Yin–Yang because there is mutual sexual tension that is mutually satisfied, and thus no Yang without Yin, or Yin without Yang.

Those who bifurcate reality into two oppositional forces, the good and the bad, fail to see that without dark there is no light, and without light there is no dark. The two are intrinsically meaningless without each other. How can there be good if there is no evil, or conversely? "You are a bad person" and "I am a good person" are simplistic renditions of reality since there is good and bad in us all. Demanding perfection of your beloved is to fail to realize that perfection is the absence of imperfection, so that without imperfection the idea of perfection would not make sense. Life and death are a continuum. With life comes death, and with death comes life. It would be impossible to speak of life without death, or death without life.

There are shades of Yin–Yang as one fades into the other. Day gradually turns into night, and night into day. The colors of the rainbow are blends of each other; there is no separation of reality into opposites that do not include each other.

Loving another is not possible without the capacity to love oneself, and loving oneself is not possible without the capacity to love another. So that narcissists, who lack the capacity to love others, cannot truly love themselves; and selfless individuals, who lack the capacity to love themselves, cannot truly love others. So, self-regard and regard for others are not opposites but, instead, are mutually supportive. One without the other is not possible. False bifurcations of these elements of human relationships lead to dysfunctionality—the selfless person who torments themselves and lives unhappily for others, or the narcissistic person who alienates others and lives unhappily without others. In contrast, the combined Yin–Yang of love for self and others makes possible an enduring love.

Such a love is also strengthened by challenges that are overcome through mutual efforts. As a young couple, in our early years of marriage, I, my wife, and infant child lived below the poverty line and confronted unemployment. We barely had enough money to buy formula to feed our child, let alone feed ourselves. On top of that, I lost my father to a massive heart attack. In our struggle, we relied on each other to get through it all.

There was hardship but there was also peace of mind in knowing that we were in it together. The Yin of agitation and the Yang of serenity were both present in our subjective lives, coalescing, harmonizing, unifying us as one, strengthening our love, commitment, and determination. True, it could have broken our spirits, and led us to drift apart. But the Yin that pushed against us, led us to push back even harder together (the Yang), thereby creating a harmonious alignment of forces that was impossible without both forces acting on each other. I do not doubt that our ability to cope with other challenges we later confronted, as a couple, was due to the unifying forces of Yin–Yang, in those early years, that strengthened our resolve and helped to plant the seeds of an enduring, romantic love.

Your existence precedes your essence

An enduring and romantic love involves intimacy. Intimacy involves emotional connectivity, which means the capacity to key into the emotions of another, share them, and validate them. It also involves the mutual sharing of deeply personal and private information and trust that these secrets are kept. Such a level of relating is not open to those who perceive others in terms of stereotypes. The latter are generalizations that classify people into fixed and rigid categories, according to a few attributes. Unfortunately, we may approach others, especially in meeting them for the first time, by applying stereotypes to them, and, thereby, fail to capture the unique features that make them special. According to media expert, Walter Lippmann,

> For the most part we do not first see, and then define, we define first and then see. In the great blooming, buzzing confusion of the outer world we pick out what our culture has already defined for us, and we tend to perceive that which we have picked out in the form stereotyped for us by our culture (loc. 963–965).

For example, we may come to hold certain fixed and rigid characterizations of people, according to their race, gender, religion, or sexual orientation. Often these generalizations are unflattering and even offensive ("All men are after just one thing"). Lippmann maintains that the tendency to construct such predefinitions is a human, self-protective mechanism. This allows us to gauge how to respond to others, in advance, especially in meeting them for the first time, so that there are no surprises for which we are not prepared. So, stereotyping is not something that only some of us do; it is, rather, something we all tend to do to one extent or another. While my stereotypes may be different from yours, we all tend to construct and apply them to one extent or other.

However, some people tend to rely more on stereotypes than others and are reticent to let their guard down, even after they have come to know others. One client repeatedly told me that, "All women are too emotional," and, as a result, encountered issues forging long-term relationships with women. Further, each time a woman cried or got upset, he used this as evidence to prove that he was correct. On the other hand, when a woman did not respond emotionally to a situation, he ignored this evidence to the contrary. Sadly, this individual had problems forging intimate relationships with women because part of intimacy is emotional connection. However, each time a women spoke about her feelings to this client, he perceived this as further confirmation that women were, after all, too emotional.

Have stereotypes of one sort or another prevented you from having intimate relationships? You may not even be aware of some of the ways stereotypes upon which you rely may be undermining your capacity for intimacy. So how can you overcome the tendency to stereotype?

Sartre (2007) provides a helpful way to think about all human beings, including ourselves. For all of us, he states, "existence precedes essence." What does this mean? It means, he says, that

> man first exists: he materializes in the world, encounters himself, and only afterward defines himself. If man as existentialists conceive of him cannot be defined, it is because to begin with he is nothing. He will not be anything until later, and then he will be what he makes of himself (p. 22).

As such, people are not like manufactured objects, such as a paper cutter, which is made with a particular purpose, which it fulfills throughout its existence. In contrast, we humans do not have a preestablished essence, a set of properties that define who we are and how we spend our time on earth. Instead, we are born without any such nature, and we freely define who we become, as guided by the decisions that we make throughout our existences. Thus, unlike a paper cutter, our existence (life) precedes our essence (purpose).

So, it is misguided to pigeon-hole human beings into fixed and rigid categories (stereotypes) and then treat them as though they had such limited capacities. When you see a paper cutter, you immediately see it in terms of this limited function. When you see your partner, do you see them in a similar limited manner, or do you see a free, autonomous person whose purposes are self-determined and thus open-ended? "The place of a woman is in the home" is a traditional stereotype that still has not lost its oppressive roots in subjugation of women, even in contemporary times. Forcing a woman to bear a child, even one conceived through rape or incest, is an example of such oppression still in vogue today. Seeing the LGBTQ community as abominations of human nature is a further example. Seeing males who are emotional (for example, cry), or are nurturers, as not being "real men" is still another.

In enduring love, partners perceive and treat each other as autonomous individuals rather than fixed stereotypes. They do not force each other to assume social roles with which they are uncomfortable, but, instead, work out divisions of labor, and life roles, with which they are comfortable. Of course, there are compromises along the way to create a viable division of labor, but there are not, nor should there be, wholesale sacrifices.

It used to be expected that, in heterosexual relationships, the wife would support her husband if he chose to go to school to earn a degree, and she would sacrifice her own education because it was more important for the man to be educated first. This is an example of stereotypical (and oppressive) thinking. Neither partner is more important than the next. All human beings, regardless of their race, gender, religion, ethnicity, or sexual orientation, have an equal right to an education and to seek their own self-actualization, as they autonomously define it.

Stereotypes prevent couples from seeing each other as they are, unique in their own special ways. If you see your partner as "the inferior sex," you will also tend to see their perspectives on the affairs of life as inferior. Your partner will, in turn, feel discounted and resent it. While the animosity may not be immediately expressed, it will be there, hidden beneath the veil of an oppressive stereotype, boiling over, from time to time, in dysphoric moods and apparently groundless emotional outbursts or nastiness. Almost assuredly, the latter will then be perceived by the other partner as further confirmation of their inferiority. Easy to dust the reality under the rug rather than to face the fact that your relationship is tainted by rigid stereotypes that usurp the prospect of an enduring, romantic love.

In the bedroom, the stereotype of male dominion plays out in its somber, unforgiving, dismal tone in traditional heterosexual relationships. The woman is expected to please "her man," while the latter stands in ultimate judgment over her performance, even though she may make her own sexual preferences known, say by placing his hand in her erogenous zone, thereby enabling her to "put out" *for him*. The deep reciprocal sharing and unifying coalescence of two souls as one never reaches climax, despite mutual orgasmic stimulation. In its stead, is the corpse of feigned lovemaking, mechanical and devoid of spirit, purely physical, pumping out bodily fluids, the scent of which conceals the stereotypical stench, much like an air freshener in a rental car that wreaks of steal cigarette smoke.

It never feels quite right, for either partner. He wants it to be better but does not really know what is missing; and she wants his approval in discharge of her wifely duty, while she silently imagines a secret lover who worships and adores her in the truest ways. Both partners are enslaved by their reciprocal stereotypes, playing out, *ad nauseam*, over a lifetime of unrequited lovemaking.

Attaining "pure awareness" of the sensory world instead of evaluating or judging it

According to the ancient Yoga sage, Patanjali (2003), "The causes of suffering are not seeing things as they are," but instead getting wrapped up in "the sense of 'I', attachment, aversion, and clinging to life" (sutra 2.3). That is, when *you* become the focus—your desires, fears, demands, etc.—you lose your ability to simply observe things as they truly are. By learning to simply observe the sensory world, without reacting to it ("How horrible!"), you can, thereby, attain "pure awareness" where you are no longer dragged along by the illusions of your material senses. "When one is unattached [...] the seeds of suffering wither, and pure awareness knows it stands alone" (sutra 3.51).

So, the goal, according to Patanjali, is to become a detached spectator of the sensory world, not a participant in it, where you are sucked into it by your own feelings. So, you observe these feelings instead of interpreting them, according to your own desires, fears, values or demands. Suppose your partner is expressing their dissatisfaction with you. You listen to what they are saying without reacting to it. You may feel agitated if they are criticizing you. But, instead of turning your feelings into catastrophic or damning declarations and actions, you simply observe these feelings. Instead of allowing yourself to be dragged into a sparring match, where you attempt to defend yourself, or become the aggressor, you allow your feelings to play out as an observer of them, not a slave to them. "I can feel the muscles in my neck tighten, a rapid heartbeat, the sense of nervous tension permeating my consciousness." You stick to this internal description of your feelings without outwardly projecting them onto your partner, blaming or damning them, or otherwise judging them—"How can they be so unkind to me!"

How many times have you become infuriated and said and done things on the spur of the moment that you have later regretted when your feelings calm down? It leaves a bitter aftertaste because you cannot take back everything you said in the heat of the moment. True love is not brittle; it does not break into pieces with an occasional loss of objectivity and control. However, a pattern of the latter can wear down the prospects of attaining an enduring love. Partners become hardened to one another's mistreatment, eventually, and drift apart. You can stop this progression by becoming a better observer, and less of a reactor.

This is not easy when the reactionary pattern has been set over a long period of time. However, making headway toward "pure awareness" is still possible. Patanjali's antidote is *mindfulness meditation*, whereby you practice focusing on your breathing or some other internal feeling, simply observing it. You then gently push negative thoughts away, allowing them to pass out of your mind just as they have entered it. Thus, you might imagine the top of your head opening and these thoughts simply floating off, or any other imagery that works for you. The goal is nonjudgmentally observing your mental content because it is the negative evaluation of life events, not their description, that leads to catastrophizing. The latter, in turn, generates intense stress, loss of intimacy, and, hence, impaired potential for building an enduring, romantic love.

Identifying Some Core Philosophical Aspects of Courage

The foregoing philosophies of objectivity and foresightedness, collectively, can help you to make more rational assessments about reality and predictions about the future, which means more enlightened judgments about danger and risk. This can, in turn, help you to avoid catastrophizing and build courage. Accordingly, core philosophical aspects of objectivity and foresightedness have been included along with core philosophical aspects of courage in the below set of philosophies:

- Courage is demonstrated, not simply in heroic deeds, but in everyday life where you modulate fear, in terms of what is reasonable under the circumstances.
- Loving someone means learning to read this person: understanding your lover's thoughts, feelings, desires, values, bodily expression, and how they are likely to perceive a situation. Such knowledge increases your ability to act courageously by showing you how to navigate your relationship: what to fear, what not to fear, what is likely to matter, what is likely not to matter, what is rash or cowardly.
- Such knowledge also includes knowing what is in your power to control and what is not. What is in your control are your own thoughts, feelings, desires, and actions. What is not in your control are those of others, or the accidents of life such as sickness. So, it is futile to make yourself anxious or depressed

over the latter things, which only places an unnecessary and self-defeating strain on your relationship.
- Hard times can bring a couple closer together. When both partners feel that they are in it together and, accordingly, work harmoniously together to overcome their life challenges, the result is likely to be increased solidarity, and hence increased likelihood of finding enduring, romantic love.
- Relationships that prosper are ones that are based on a commitment to mutual welfare and the prosperity of the relationship itself. This commitment means knowing about what conduces to such welfare and prosperity. It entails the willpower to act accordingly, taking risks when the stakes warrant taking them under the circumstances. Courage is always exercised in given contexts, so absolutistic, unconditional patterns of responding are not likely to conduce to enduring love.
- Taking risks is part of courageously acting, but the risks should be reasonable, or at least not unreasonable. Courageous lovers do not throw themselves into the proverbial fire unless there is good reason supported by evidence.
- Risks are a part of the human condition. Even in not acting, you are still taking risks. In love, there are always risks, but there are also always risks in never committing to love. Only in the former case, however, is there a chance of finding romantic love.
- Certainty is not in the cards, for the empirical universe is always uncertain. But certainty is boring and, without risks, there would be no challenges, and thus no triumphs. The labors of love would be meaningless since the results would be guaranteed anyway.
- It's not about certainty, but instead *probabilities*. The world of everyday life is one of possibilities, chances to one degree or another. Whatever door one opens, there is also likely to be other doors, and other choices to make. Experience can give us cues as to which doors to open but it never tells us what to do. So, how to choose is an eternal question.
- Fortunately, there are ways to increase your foresightedness, although you will never be omniscient, for the future is always uncertain. Seeing that things have consistently gone together in the past increases the probability that they will go together again in the future.
- Reasoning by analogy can also be useful. Seeing that A and B are alike in several ways makes it more probable that they will resemble each other in further ways. That you and your date both share interests in literature, have similar political perspectives, and are both musicians, increases the probability that you will enjoy each other's company. However, the fact that you enjoy an

active lifestyle, while your date is a homebody, diminishes the probability that you will enjoy each other's company.
- Trust is not blind. It is based on evidence, which increases over the months and years of an ongoing relationship, but never reaches certainty. Still, in true love, the preponderance of evidence consistently supports trust, which morphs into a deep faith in the beloved, which endows true love with its aura of sanctity. But, again, this trust is continuously tested over time. Transgression at an advanced stage is, therefore, a deep personal, almost unthinkable lose.
- Love is a balance of joy and sadness. Tension is a precursor to resolution. Without the former, there could not exist the latter; without darkness there could be no light; so that the bifurcations of reality (one or the other but not both) are likely to be oversimplified. Relationships thrive on such polarities. In sexual love, it is not about my sexual gratification or yours (exclusively); it is about both. More exactly, it is about the unified, seamless amalgamation of both.
- Strife and tranquility are not mutually exclusive; for the greatest love arises from both, where a couple works together to overcome strife, and, consequently, finds peace and tranquility in love.
- Stereotyping your partner ("You're a bossy woman, so something must be wrong with you," "You're just a man, so how can you understand how I really feel," "Can't teach an old dog new tricks") blocks the intimacy required for cultivating enduring, romantic love. This means that, instead of seeing your partner as a unique individual, you perceive a fixed and rigid category and fail to connect with the person. But people are not like manufactured objects whose "essences" are pre-established, and thus limited. Couples can grow and flourish together, and become who they autonomously seek to be, together as a couple, and individually, as distinct, unique individuals.
- Human beings tend to think in terms of "I," "me," and "mine" so that you say, "I am feeling sad," "This is hurtful to me," and "This is mine." But what happens if you detach the sense impressions you receive from the "I," "me," and "mine" and see them as they are, apart from relating them to you in these ways? This would give you "pure awareness" of the sensory world. It would make you an objective observer rather than a self-interested one. It would transcend your own values, desires, and aversions that you attach to the sensory world, such that you no longer react (negatively or positively) to it, and, thus, avoid being distracted by your own interests.

- Such a perspective could enable you to relate to your partner, without judging them: to listen to them, without adding your own self-interested twist, to see them as they are, without damning or criticizing them, and to have feelings or sensations, including pain, without catastrophizing about it. In this frame of mind, you no longer suffer. Your partner does not disturb you; they are no longer a problem to be solved; what they say or feel is clear, without having injected yourself into its meaning or significance. In this frame of mind, feelings of loving kindness and compassion for your partner freely arise, without their being "dragged along" by focusing on yourself rather than your partner.

Applying the Eclectic Philosophy through Cognitive–Behavioral Practice

Applying the foregoing philosophical ideas means practicing them, which involves using them to build courage and the related virtues of foresightedness and objectivity. You can work toward this goal by engaging in the cognitive–behavioral activities suggested in Exercises 1 and 2 and applying the Guidelines I have provided for practicing these virtues in your everyday life.

EXERCISE 1

Risk-Taking Exercise

Taking rational risks is part of building courage and cultivating an exciting, creative, love life. This does not mean doing things that are likely to defeat your purposes (for example, buying a home that you can't afford).

1. Do something that does not have unreasonable risks. Choose something that you would like to do but have been afraid to do. For example, this might be trying something new in bed, moving in with your partner, or proposing. It could be something you have wanted to tell your partner that you have been afraid to say for fear of being negatively judged but think your partner should know about you. Alternatively, you can do something outside the relationship such as applying for a new job, going back to school, or something else you wanted to do but haven't gotten up the willpower to do. What you choose can be a solo act or it can be something you do cooperatively

---

(*Continued*)

with your partner. It does not have to be something big. Start small and work up to bigger things. For example, if you and your partner have always wanted to take dancing lessons but you believe you have two left feet, then you can start by taking dancing lessons.
2. Deal with the consequences. Because you cannot be certain of the outcome of your risk-taking behavior, be prepared to cope with the consequences in case it does not work out as you hoped. This means applying some of the philosophies from this chapter (or other chapters) to reframe the results. For example, you can apply Popper's scientific approach to see the results as an opportunity to learn from your mistakes. Alternatively, you can take Nietzsche's approach in seeing the results as an opportunity for you, individually or as a couple, to grow stronger through the experience.

EXERCISE 2

Avoiding Stereotypes

All of us stereotype, so what are your stereotypes? Are you stereotyping your partner in some way? For example, do you have cultural blinders on regarding gender, age, sexual orientation, race, religion, ethnicity, or another generic category? We may not always be aware that we are stereotyping someone. This exercise is intended to help you identify and avoid stereotypes you may be applying to your partner.

1. Makes three lists of your partner's individual traits. In the first list, include his positive traits (very intelligent, good in bed, affectionate [...]). In the second list, include his negative traits (impatient, moodiness, leaves the toilet seat up [...]); and in the third list, include his quirks (likes to eat raw onions like they were apples, is ambidextrous, becomes beat red when embarrassed [...]). This can help you relate to your partner as a unique individual instead of a fixed, rigid stereotype.
2. Reflect on what you have discovered about your partner by compiling your lists. Do you tend to think of your partner in terms of one or few fixed character traits (in other words in terms of a stereotype) rather than as a distinct individual with many different characteristics?

Guidelines for building courage, foresightedness, and objectivity

- Show courage daily, by listening to constructive feedback from your partner, pertaining to your relationship, and providing such feedback to your partner, even though this may not be easy to do.
- Know your partner. Attend to their body language. The nuanced inflections in their voice can tell you much about what they are thinking but not saying. Observe their facial expressions; the lifting of an eyebrow when they are not being entirely honest with you. Note the positioning of their body—leaning forward when they are engaged, or backward when disengaged. Gather more information from your partner by asking open-ended questions such as "How do you feel?" or "What do you think?"), rather than closed-ended ones such as "Are you okay?" or "Do you agree?"
- Ask yourself, "Is this something I can change, such as my own thoughts, feelings, or actions?" If the answer is yes, then rationally consider making the change. If the answer is no, then don't disturb yourself about it because this would be self-defeating.
- Thus, in challenging times, practice courage by remaining calm and deliberative, neither over- nor under-reacting, and by consoling your loved ones; for these things are in your power.
- Find ways to relieve unnecessary emotional stress. For example, lovemaking can be a powerful way for you and your partner to build solidarity in confronting life challenges together.
- More generally, reframe the mundane challenges and strife of everyday life (from job security to illness) as opportunities to exercise courage, build character, and become more unified as a couple.
- Exercise courage by *acting* on your considered judgments. Suppose you and your partner are deciding about whether to get pregnant. "Is it the right time?" "Can we afford to care for a child?" "Are we both prepared to be parents?" Avoid overthinking (or under-thinking) these questions. Avoid creating dilemmas ("If we have a child, we won't be able to afford it; and if we don't, we will forever regret it. Damned if we do and damned if we don't!"). Base your decision on the evidence, not on fear or catastrophizing "It will be challenging but I am getting my degree and should be able to find work."
- Don't procrastinate. Inaction also has consequences! You will never be certain. Embrace probability, instead, by proportioning the degree of risk to what is at stake, based on your priorities (or those of your partner). For example, a medical procedure with a 2% mortality risk may be worth the risk for you if

there is a 99% risk of paralysis without the procedure and ambulation is a priority for you.
- Don't keep doing the same thing if it hasn't worked in the past. So, for example, if your sexual relationship has become humdrum, try different sexual activities that you both might find gratifying. Again, don't demand certainty, but things are not likely to improve unless you explore new, potentially exciting activities. This applies outside the bedroom too!
- Increase the range of activities you do together that you both enjoy. This means sitting down and discussing new possibilities to add more pizazz to your relationship. Increasing your common enjoyments will not guarantee that your relationship will succeed, but it will greatly increase the probability that it will.
- Honesty is the progenitor of trust. Be honest and forthright with your partner *as a rule.* This does not mean you should not exercise discretion, in not saying things that are poorly timed or likely to more harm than good to your relationship. This may not always be easy, but, oftentimes, it is not the things that you hide that are most damaging but rather the fact that you have hidden them. Making decisions that affect both of you, without first discussing them with your partner, is likely to damage your relationship. Keep at the forefront of your mind that enduring love thrives on candor, which builds trust.
- Taking your love for granted is a grandiose mistake. True love is reaffirmed daily in reciprocal caring and being there for each other. It is inscribed in declaring your love for one another by regularly uttering the words, "I love you," and in making love on a consistent basis. How often should you make love? This is to be mutually agreed upon, however you both should consistently make time for it, and it should be considered an essential part of your relationship, not something optional to be postponed or put off.
- Do not be afraid of conflict. If you and your lover disagree, this is an occasion to talk about it, work it through, or seek a resolution. It is almost always self-defeating to conceal your disagreement just to avoid conflict. Such concealment continues to brew beneath the surface, and leads to resentment, alienation, and loss of trust. Sometimes agreeing to disagree is a reasonable approach; other times, there is room for compromise; other times, for the sake of addressing an issue, deference can be reasonable. Conflict is often an opportunity to receive useful feedback. Being open to conflict is therefore extremely important on route to an enduring love.
- This does not mean that it is okay to engage in shouting matches, name-calling, blame games, or other modes of disrespectful relating. The latter is counterproductive and breeds hard feelings. A respectful civil tongue is more

likely to yield productive results. Some couples engage in such self-defeating banter before they sit down and speak respectfully. This can become a bad habit. Practice cutting to the chase and engaging each other civilly, instead.
- Try to gain "pure awareness" of your partner and others in your life instead of judging them through "I," "me," and "mine." You can do this by practicing your mindfulness (see Chapter 1).

The above guidelines, regularly practiced, can help you address the tendency to catastrophize about the perceived challenges and potential challenges of life by developing foresightedness to rationally assess risks, based on the evidence. They can foster objectivity to accurately assess reality without oversimplifying it; and courage to modulate fear, in proportion to such rational risk and reality assessments, and to act accordingly.

Catastrophizing, however, is one tip of the iceberg that can sink the love boat. Indeed, partners who catastrophize typically demand perfection, ego-obsess, damn themselves or others, and/or exhibit lack of self-control. So, working on cultivating enduring, romantic love involves working on all the other impediments addressed in this book.

As you have seen, the therapy developed here systematically addresses all six interrelated impediments by applying the wisdom of the ages to cultivate lovable virtues of courage, serenity, self-control, respect, and empathy, among others. In the next (and final) chapter of this book, romantic love, and its implications for your sex life are summed up.

References

American Psychological Association. n.d. "What is Exposure Therapy?" Clinical Practice Guidelines for the Treatment of Post-Traumatic Stress Disorder. https://www.apa.org/ptsd-guideline/patients-and-families/exposure-therapy.

Aristotle. 1941. "Nicomachean Ethics." Trans. W. D. Ross. In *The Basic Works of Aristotle*, ed. by Richard McKeon, 930–1112. New York: Random House.

Aurelius, Marcus. 2001. *Meditations*. Project Gutenberg eBook. https://www.gutenberg.org/cache/epub/2680/pg2680-images.html.

Emerson, Ralph Waldo. 1904. "Courage." In *The Complete Works*, vol. 7. Boston: Houghton Mifflin. https://quod.lib.umich.edu/cgi/t/text/text-idx?c=emerson;cc=emerson;view=toc;idno=4957107.0007.001.

Lao-Tzu. 2017. *Tao Te Ching: An Insightful and Modern Translation*, Trans. J. H. McDonald. Qigong Vacations.org.

Lippmann, Walter. 2004. *Public Opinion*. Project Gutenberg eBook. https://www.gutenberg.org/ebooks/6456.

Mill, John Stuart. 2009. *A System of Logic, Ratiocinative and Inductive*. Project Gutenberg eBook. https://www.gutenberg.org/cache/epub/27942/pg27942-images.html.
Patanjali. 2003. *The Yoga-Sutra of Pantanjali: Sanskrit-English Translation & Glossary*, Trans. Chip Hartranft. Internet Archives. https://archive.org/details/chip-hartranft-sanskrit-english-translation-glossary-the-yoga-sutra-of-patanjali/mode/2up.
Russell, Bertrand. 1972. *The Problems of Philosophy*. London: Oxford University Press.
Sartre, Jean-Paul. 2007. *Existentialism is a Humanism*, Trans. Carol Macomber. New Haven: Yale University Press (Kindle ed.). https://www.amazon.com/Existentialism-Humanism-Jean-Paul-Sartre/dp/0300115466.
University of Colorado at Boulder. 2018, December 10. "Your Brain on Imagination: It's A Lot Like Reality, Study Shows," Science Daily. https://www.sciencedaily.com/releases/2018/12/181210144943.htm#:~:text=Summary%3A,phobias%20or%20post%20traumatic%20stress.

CHAPTER 6

THE IDEAL OF ENDURING LOVE AND SEXUAL INTIMACY

> Sex is central to intimacy as its medium of expression [...] Intimacy in turn is central to love as that set of essentially private and personal roles through which we build a shared identity [...]
>
> —Robert Solomon, *Love: Emotion, Myth, and Metaphor*

Enduring Love and Sexual Intimacy in Theory and Practice

Sexual attraction brings us together, like other creatures in the animal kingdom, but this is only the beginning. As you have seen, it takes time, patience, and perseverance to cultivate love that lasts and has the magnificent valence of true love. It is like a fine wine, growing finer with age. There is, however, no ultimate orgasm, just as there is no perfect wine. The process of enduring romantic love begins here on earth, and where it ends—here on earth or in heaven—is a matter of faith. As Plato would admonish, only an imperfect copy of love is exemplified here on earth. The ideal of Love lies outside space and time, which makes it eternal and immutable. Such an ideal form thus lies outside the reach of any human being.

There is a myth that love *is* a special kind of feeling. But what feeling is this? Is it the bodily titillation you feel when you are sexually aroused? This would make true love the same as the product of sexual stimulation, which would mean a one-night stand, rich in multiple, intense orgasms, or perhaps an all-night orgy, could produce true love. Veritably, sexual feelings are a part of romantic love, but it would be worse than a half-truth to say that true love, itself, is a sexual feeling.

As has been emphasized here, having sex, and making love are not the same thing. The uninitiated think they are because they have never experienced true romantic love. The sexual organism can be intensely pleasurable, but it is far different when it comingles and coalesces with the deep, ever-evolving, committed caring that characterizes true love. Focusing on the sexual aspect commits a fallacy of composition because the whole is greater, infinitely greater, than the sum of the parts.

"My life is incomplete without you" can be a sign that one is needy and not necessarily that one is in love. So, you may feel lost without this person because you have become accustomed to having them as your support system. This is not necessarily true love; for true lovers, as you have seen, are independent and autonomous persons who come together for a "more perfect" union, although such a union, as said, is ever-evolving and never perfect.

This does not mean that lovers do not lean on each other for support. Indeed, this is what the vows of marriage allude to when it is said, "for better or for worse, in sickness and in health." Being there in time of need is not optional in true love. It is part of what deep caring in love means. But this does not mean that love is a relationship of overdependency. It is far more functional than that.

Two lovers bring to the relationship something of their own that forms an incommensurably valuable unity. It is like taking two precious metals and combining them so that they form something far more precious.

There is no lip service in true love because it is authentic and real. True lovers do not feign love; they live in and for it. The two hearts that beat as one do not necessarily both die when one of those hearts stops beating, although it sometimes does. Just witness the couple who have been together in love for 60 years wherein the one dies shortly after the other, even minutes apart. This is no coincidence because there is such synergy, like a fine-tuned machine that suddenly breaks down in one place, and, as a result, crashes in another.

As you have seen, love can be painful; it can hurt because you have given your lover the power to break your heart. This is especially true if you assume that true love must be perfect. Then you will, assuredly, be distraught when your true lover (eventually) lets you down. However, mistakes, which are invariably made in the best of relationships, are not necessarily a bad thing and can even strengthen the relationship.

As you have also seen, conflict can be a good thing in a devoted relationship because it is a sign that there is, then, the opportunity to work through one's differences in a candid manner, which builds trust and solidarity. Too little disclosure or conflict is as bad as too much. True love needs work when devoted partners are in combat mode far too frequently to build virtuous habits of serenity and peace of mind, which habits are part of enduring, romantic love.

Virtues, as said, consist of good habits, which means that they are *tendencies or dispositions* to act, feel, and think in ways that are conducive to happiness. As such, they allow for sailing off course now and then, but when sailing off course itself becomes a habit, then shipwreck is the likely consequence, sooner rather than later.

The role of philosophical ideas in building enduring, romantic love has been a vital theme in this book. The power of philosophy lies in its incredible capacity to lift the soul, to bring the abstract to bear on the concrete. In my clinical practice, I have seen so many people find consolation in a philosophical reframing of a problem of living that removes the issue from the realm of gloom and doom to an occasion for growing stronger or making constructive change.

As you have seen, Eastern philosophies such as Daoism conceive of reality in terms of Yin and Yang and make the incredibly important point that there is a Yin in every Yang, and a Yang in every Yin (Lao-Tzu, 2017). Relationships that suffer from boredom are prime candidates for becoming exciting, wherein the initial boringness of the relationship sets the glorious background for the excitement to follow. Did you before consider that the boredom you may now be experiencing can be the minerals that can help nourish and give vitality back to your relationship? It's sometimes hard to see such reframes when one's head is buried in the proverbial sand.

Have you been persistently making the same mistake, repeatedly, *ad nauseam*, by trying to control other people's lives, especially your loved ones? The Stoics have admonished us not to try to control what is not in our power to control. Voila, a very simple insight. Right? But have you considered that this is what you have mindlessly been attempting to do without any success and with great frustration?

Existentialists like Sartre, Camus, Kierkegaard, and Heidegger, among others, have been very blunt about one's freedom and responsibility to shape one's own life, including one's love life. But, while some may bow their heads in agreement with this philosophy, once it is pointed out, have they been applying it to their own lives? How many, instead, play the blame game, blaming their partners for the things that routinely go wrong rather than accepting their freedom and responsibility to choose a different approach? Have you been living in "bad faith" by telling yourself that you are the victim of circumstances? Have you been telling yourself that you have no options left; that the cards have been stacked against you; that your life would be perfect if only others would leave you alone? Take heed of the philosophical message that admonishes you against such counterproductive thinking and *do* something about it.

Philosophies are not, *by themselves*, going to change your life. As has been emphasized in this book, they are as good as you are willing to apply them to your life. This is why I have taken much effort to draw out, in practical terms, many of the cognitive–behavioral implications that follow from the various eclectic philosophies presented here. It is so that you can put them to work in your everyday life. Without such practice, these philosophies are like crude oil in the ground. They have much potential but, unless they are refined and harnessed, they are of little extrinsic value.

So, you will need to practice your loveable philosophy, not just accept it on an intellectual level; internalize it emotionally too, *by living it*. The value is incommensurable, but the effort must be consistent and persistent. The good news is that, if you are reading this last chapter, after having read through the entirety of this book, performed the exercises, and worked on following the guidelines, you have already made headway to an enduring, romantic love.

Be careful about clichés, such as "It takes two to Tango," however. Yes, your partner is also part of the mix. However, modeling rational philosophies, rather than throwing in the towel when you see that your partner is resistant to change, is not a good idea. Again, it takes time and perseverance. Oftentimes, constructive change in relationships follows only after things get worse. How so?

Imagine you are no longer falling into the trap of bickering endlessly with your partner after years of having done so. Your partner perceives a difference in how you are responding to them and tries even harder to engage you—maybe by calling you a name that they know you especially loathe. After all, this is a nasty habit that has crystallized over many years, so how can you expect your partner to respond any differently to your disengagement? So, your partner doubles down, and your relationship gets even rockier.

Are you going to continue to be codependent and lapse into the same routine, or are you going to persist in rational behavior? This is the hardest part, but it is an obstacle you will invariably need to get over to make constructive changes and set your path toward enduring, romantic love. It is quite possible (although, as emphasized, not certain) that your partner will, eventually, begin to change for the better. This change is gradual, very gradual. There are, almost definitely, going to be relapses or backsliding, but, over time, they should become fewer and fewer if it is working.

How long should you try? The answer depends on how much your relationship is worth to you. I have seen couples spend an entire lifetime wasting their potential for happiness by repeating the same fallacies—demanding perfection, catastrophizing, damning themselves and others, low frustration tolerance, etc. Either because they are codependent, and/or they are truly devoted to one another but just don't know how to change, such couples don't give up. Do they have the capacity to constructively apply the eclectic philosophies provided herein to overcome these impediments to true love? Based on my own clinical work, I believe that, in all probability, many of these couples have that capacity.

Unlovable Habits, Lovable Virtues, and Their Philosophies

Cultivating an enduring, romantic love is about exchanging bad habits for good ones. You now have a handle on some of the most serious impediments to such true love. You are not expected to *always* act, think, and feel in lovable ways. As stressed in this book, human beings, not even very accomplished lovers, are perfect. So, the goal is to work toward constant improvement in your relationship. This is important because you should not be discouraged when your relationship encounters troubled waters, as invariably it will, going forward. The point is to recognize where the problem lies. Which of the impediments are rocking the boat? Which lovable virtues are, therefore, at stake; and which philosophical ideas would be helpful to apply to quell the storm?

This does not mean that you won't, subsequently, encounter challenges in your relationship. Indeed, the tides are always changing, and it is inevitable that you and your partner will wrestle with further challenges on your life journey together. But this is truly what makes life so exciting. If everything went smoothly and there were no challenges, life would be boring. Part of the excitement of forging ahead toward enduring, romantic love is that it is a delicate, fragile thing of beauty that constantly requires attention for its continual nourishment. If it came easy, it would not be so precious. If diamonds were like raindrops, you would not care much, if at all, if you lost one. But true love is rare, and it also requires a lot of maintenance and a lot of tender loving care. So, when you have a burgeoning true love, be mindful of what a marvelous, precious thing you have. Nurture and take care of it, as though it were a newborn child needing constant attention, keeping in mind the incredible potential it has for bringing so much happiness to the both of you.

The lovable virtues are aspirational goals that provide guiding lights toward enduring, romantic love. For couples whose relationships are in peril, they are like the lighthouse that provides direction toward land for the ship lost at sea. Your willpower is the wind behind the sails that can carry the ship toward its destination. But the ship needs to be steered in the right direction—toward the guiding light, the lovable virtues. This is where the philosophical ideas come in. They keep the steering wheel on its course, constantly reminding you about what is at stake. But these philosophies need to be put into action. This means that, unless you use them (apply them to your life), they will not help you reach dry land.

So, you need to put in the work. It is an important insight of current cognitive-behavioral therapy that reframing your thinking will not lead to constructive change unless you also put your actions behind your new way of thinking. Realizing that calling your partner derogatory names is counterproductive will not make a difference if you don't change your behavior too.

As discussed in Chapter 4, psychologists refer to this state of intellectual appreciation as *cognitive dissonance*. This is when you know what is rational but persist in your irrational behavior. Cognitive dissonance is a part of the process of constructive change because you are not likely to change if you don't know what you need to change. So, constructive change begins when you understand, on an intellectual level, what the impediment is to your relationship, what the virtues are toward which you should be aspiring, and what philosophical ideas can help to get you there. However, it is through actual behavioral change that you are likely to come to appreciate the latter on an *emotional* level. The latter is when you not only know that your behavior is wrong, but it also *feels* wrong. This happens when you put your rational thinking into action; for example, you stop the name-calling shenanigans.

This takes willpower, powered by respect for self and others, based on philosophical ideas that resonate: "My partner, like myself, is a person, who has intrinsic worth and dignity, who has incredible capacities to think, decide, feel, hope, desire, dream, and love, who also sometimes makes mistakes. But this does not make my partner, or myself, a mistake, or a nasty name. There's a lot more under the hood than that!"

Just Having Sex in Romantic Love

Having distinguished between making love and just having sex, I have spoken at length about engaging in the former. Let me forestall any misunderstanding. As I have stated in the Introduction, just having sex also has its place. In the early stages of any romance, one ordinarily just has sex. The bond of intimacy that comes with deep commitment and caring has not ordinarily taken shape yet and the couple is feeling its way forward, seeing if there is something special that has potential. The orgasm reached is significant because it is a physical sign, a cue of more to come. From the perspective of forging enduring romantic love, it is not an end in itself; but it is a necessary condition. If there is no physical attraction, then there is nothing to build on. But what about after a couple has found true romantic love? Is it okay to just have sex?

The answer to this question is in the affirmative. You may not always be in the mood for making love but rather feel like just having sex. To evoke, again, the analogy made in the Introduction, you may prefer a tall bottle of Bud Lime while watching the Miami Heat play. Whereas, imbibing in a vintage bottle of Domaine Leroy Musigny Grand Cru would be wasted on the game and would best be left to an intimate setting such as a candlelit table at a French café with your true love. Each may hit the spot for its specific purpose, but they are obviously not the same thing. For example, one former client, who was in a long-term, romantic love relationship with her husband, enjoyed dressing up as a prostitute, occasionally, and meeting him in a motel to have sex. The two were deeply in love, however, and often made authentic love.

As Martin Buber would remind us, you do not always speak Thou to your lover. Sometimes, your lover counts on you to carry out a task, for example, going grocery shopping, while you count on your lover to reciprocate, for example, preparing a meal. In this mode of relating, you each speak IT to one another—each of you using the other for a particular purpose. In making love, two lovers speak Thou to each other; while in just having sex each speaks IT to the other. These two modes of relating are distinct and, according to Buber, one does not relate just in one of these ways all the time.

For true lovers, just having sex necessarily leaves something to be desired. It does not quench sexual thirst. It is not that true lovers cannot get enough sex; it is rather that just having sex is limited in its capacity to satisfy one who has beheld the ineffable, magical quality of lovemaking.

Just having sex, on occasion, thus has the effect of reaffirming the inestimable worth of making love; for it is in the latter that one feels at home, coalescing, losing oneself in the other, and the other in oneself; this exquisite unifying orgasmic transcendence; the mother of all orgasms; beyond which, this side of heaven, there is nothing more sublime. So, yes, it is okay for true lovers to just have sex. No, perhaps even more than okay, just having sex can be part of the foreplay that sets the stage for the subsequent lovemaking, wherein the ultimate climax is achieved.

> **Are There Limits to Lovemaking?**
>
> In this video, I discuss whether there are limits to making love. For example, is making love consistent with sadomasochistic sex? Can there be lovemaking in a menage-a-trois? Does using pornography undermine lovemaking?
>
>
>
> https://youtu.be/nIQjKvZFYtY

The Social Scope of Making Love

This book has also emphasized that the sexual intimacy of making love cannot attain outside a loving relationship; and the latter cannot attain outside stable relationships with others such as friends, colleagues, workmates, and interactions with others in the community in which one lives. So, what happens in the bedroom is a function of a much broader system in which it is embedded. True love, that is, enduring, romantic love, does not happen in a dysfunctional life. It is perpetually nourished by the interpersonal relations one cultivates both inside and outside the intimate relationship with one's partner. Thus, overcoming the six unlovable impediments arising *outside* the bedroom (such as in the broader familial context) can be as important to functionality *inside* the bedroom as addressing these impediments arising inside it.

If you tend to demand perfection, ego-obsess, self-damn, damn others, exercise poor self-control, or catastrophize *outside* your intimate relationship with your partner, this can also impair your potential for functionality inside this relationship. Thus, dysfunction on the outside tends to breed dysfunction on the inside, including inside the bedroom, and conversely. For example, if your interpersonal relations at work suffer, because you tend to demand perfection from your coworkers, you may also demand perfection from your partner, in bed. So, addressing the root problem, that of perfectionism can have implications both inside and outside the bedroom.

Such synergy between our social selves and our private selves is remarkable. According to Aristotle (2009), there is "[a] social instinct [...] implanted in all men by nature" (Part 2). We are happy only if we cultivate relationships within our broader social environments. Couples are not likely to find true love who live in isolation from others, who shut out the rest of the world, and who live as hermits. They are not likely to find true love without friends, companions, family, and community relations, or if they live in perpetual conflict with others.

Thus, the distinction often made between public and private life should not obfuscate the truth that what goes on behind closed doors in your personal life, and what goes on outside them, are largely interdependent. In true love, there is synergy, harmony, and balance between these worlds. You feel good inside and outside your intimate relationship, and your lover feels the same too. This is a delicate and precious balance, indeed, never quite perfect.

In your journey toward enduring, romantic love, you will inevitably lose perspective now and then, and get sidetracked. However, you can get back on track by knowing where you messed up; and where you want to be; having the philosophical insight and the willpower to apply this wisdom; and having honed your skills through practice. You will, then, be set on course, toward a deeply gratifying, lifelong, ever-evolving, enduring, romantic, true love. This is a love more precious than any gem; more priceless; transcendent in beauty; divine; beyond the most beautiful sonnet that speaks to it. I wish you profound success, on your life journey, in attaining enduring love and sexual intimacy.

References

Aristotle. 2009. *Politics*. The Internet Classics Archive. http://classics.mit.edu//Aristotle/politics.html.

Lao-Tzu. 2017. *Tao Te Ching: An Insightful and Modern Translation*, Trans. J. H. McDonald. Qigong Vacations.org.

INDEX

abandonment, perceived 55
absolutistic rules, as impediments to love 99, 124, 132, *see also* demanding perfection
abstract ideas, communication of meanings in lovemaking 70
abusive relationships 56, 57
acceptance, unconditional, *see also* respect for self and others
 of life 88, 89
 of self and others 36, 43, 46, 58, 59, 64, 65, 68–74
anger, toward partner 18, 36, 41, 65, 70, 77, 84, 88, 91
anxiety, performance 25, 96
approval, demanding 29, 54–55, 94, *see also* demanding perfection
Aquinas, Thomas 66, 93
Aristotle, view of
 character 8–9
 courage 81, 112–13, 118–19
 love 5
 social instinct 149
 truth 33–34
 virtue, nature of 10, 28
Aurelius, Marcus 121, *see also* stoicism
authenticity x, xi, 4, 10, 11, 29, 142, 147
autonomy, as condition of romantic love 25, 28, 38, 59–61, 69, 72, 74, 85, 92, 116–18, 128–29, 133, 142

bandwagon thinking (blind conformity) 11, 19, *see also* authenticity
Belenky, Mary Field, *see* knowing
Browning, Elizabeth Barrett 3

Buber, Martin, on "I-It" and "I-Thou" 6–7, 61–62, 147
Buddha, *see* Buddhism
Buddhism 23, 27, 64, 65

can'tstipation
 behavioral 80–82
 cognitive 85–87
 emotional 82–84
 frustration 84–85
 types of 79
catastrophizing, *see also* courage; foresightedness; objectivity
 counteracting philosophies of 118–31
 definition of 9
 identifying counteracting virtues of 112–18
 recognizing as impediment to romantic love 109–12
certainty, demand for 20, 99–100, 114–15, 123–25, 132, 133, *see also* demanding perfection
cognitive dissonance 67, 78, 146
cognitive-behavioral approach, to building romantic love 9, 14–15, *see also* logic-based therapy
Cohen, Elliot D. 10, 12, 48, 54, 78–79, 113–14
commitment, in loving relationships xi, 1–4, 36, 42–43, 79, 113, 122–23, 125, 127, 132, 146–47
constructive change, five-step method of 12, *see also* logic-based therapy
control, demanding 19, *see also* demanding perfection; Epictetus

151

courage, *see also* Aristotle, view of, courage; catastrophizing
   core philosophical aspects of 131–34
   counteracting behavioral *can't*stipation with 92–93
   definition of 11
   guidelines for building 136–38
   philosophies of 99–102, 112–14, 118–22

Dalai Lama x, 42, 53, 65
Damasio, Antonio 83
damning others, *see also* respect for self and others
   description of 9
   as impediment to romantic love 55–57
damning self, *see also* respect for self and others
   description of 9
   as impediment to romantic love 53–55
de Beauvoir, Simone x, 38, 49
decisiveness, *see* self-control, identifying virtues of
demanding perfection, *see also* serenity
   description of 9
   as impediment to romantic love 18–22, 99
depression 36, 87
Derrida, Jacque, and deconstruction of oppositional hierarchies 26–27
Descartes, Rene 39, 40, 44, 63

eclectic philosophy 13, 14, 28–29, 46–48, 71–72, 74, 104, 134–35, 144, 145
ecstatic sex, in making love 6, 15, 23, 58
ego-obsessing, description of 9, *see also* ego-obsessiveness, as impediment to romantic love
ego-obsessiveness, as impediment to romantic love 33–34, *see also* empathy
Ellis, Albert, view of unconditional acceptance of self and others 58, 59, 64
empathy, *see also* ego-obsessiveness, as impediment to romantic love
   core philosophical aspects of 45–46
   as counteractive to ego-obsessiveness 34–37
   definition of 11
   guidelines for building 48–50
   philosophies of 38–45
Epictetus 12, 24, 98, *see also* stoicism
Epicurus 67–68, 93, 94
erection 18, 80, 85, 91, 115

foresightedness, *see also* catastrophizing
   counteracting catastrophizing with 114–16
   definition of 11
   guidelines for building 136–38
   philosophies of 122–25
Fromm, Erich, view of love 5, 7, 57

Goldman, Alan 4
guilt 36, 54, 56, 86–88

habits, unlovable, list of with counteracting virtue 11
Holly, Buddy 2–3
Hume, David 95

Intimacy, sexual, described ix

James, William 99

Kant, Immanuel, view of
   respect for persons 13, 59–61, 93
   sexual love 5, 7
knowing
   connected 44–45
   separate 44

labels, use of derogatory 56, 73
Lao Tzu 22, 96, 125, 143
listening, active 36, 37, 49, 84, 95, 120, *see also* empathy
logic-based therapy 10
love, philosophy of, embracing 12
lovemaking
   v. just having sex 4–8
   social scope of 148–49

manipulation 25, 60, 72–73
meditation
   loving-kindness 48, 104
   mindfulness 24, 29, 48, 131
menage-a-trois 148

Index

Neo-Platonism 4, *see also* Plotinus, and ecstatic experience
Nietzsche, Fredrich 94, 101, 135

objectivity, *see also* catastrophizing
   core philosophical aspects of 131–34
   definition of 11
   guidelines for building 136–38
   overcoming catastrophizing with 116–18
   philosophies of 125–31

Patanjali 43, 98, 130
patiences and perseverence, *see* self-control, identifying virtues of
philosophical ideas, role in building romantic love xi, 12, 14–15, 134, 143, 145, 146
Plato, view of
   love 5–6, 50, 141
   perfection and imperfection 25–27
Plotinus, and ecstatic experience 4, 58
poor self-control, *see also* self-control
   description of 9
   as impediment to romantic love 77–87

rational-emotive imagery 12, 30
reflection 37, *see also* listening, active
reframing, of a problem 9, 11, 13, 20–21, 59, 143, 146
respect for self and others, *see also* damning others; damning self
   core philosophical aspects of 69–70
   as counters to self-and other-damnation 57–59
   descriptions of 11
   guidelines for building 72–75
   philosophies of 59–68
Rogers, Carl R. 34–35, 59, *see also* acceptance, unconditional, of self and others
romantic love, as distinguished from other types of love ix–x

sadomasochistic sex 60–61, 148
Santayana, George 40
Sartre, Jean-Paul
   on creating life plans 63, 94, 123, 128, 143
   and precariousness of life 99–100

self-control
   core philosophical aspects of, 102–4
   description of, 11
   guidelines for building, 105–6
   identifying virtues of, 87–93
   philosophies of, 93–101
self-damning, *see* damning self
serenity, *see also* demanding perfection
   core philosophical aspects of 27–28
   as counter to demanding perfection 20–22
   description of 11
   philosophies of 22–27
sex
   dysfunctional 18
   orgasmic 4, 7, 8, 18, 60–61, 81, 110, 129, 147
Shakespeare, William 7, 11, 109
shame-attacking exercise 29, 72
stereotypes 118, 127–30, 135
stoicism 12, 24, 29, 98, 121–22, 143
systems approach, to building romantic love 10, 149

Taoism 27, *see also* Lao Tzu
temperance, *see* self-control, identifying virtues of
Thich Nhat Hahn 41, 95

unlovable habits, *see* habits, unlovable, list of with counteracting virtue

virtues, *see also* logic-based therapy
   as aspirational goals 10, 11
   counteractive nature of 10
   described 4, 143
   as means between extremes 10
   as mutually supportive/interdependent 30
   practice of 10
virtues of love, nature of 10–12

willpower 11, 73, 78, 83, 105, 132, 134, 146, 149

yin and yang, *see* Lao Tzu
Yoga 44, 98, *see also* Patanjali

www.ingramcontent.com/pod-product-compliance
Lightning Source LLC
Chambersburg PA
CBHW032027230426
43671CB00005B/223